MW00862203

I hope this book will inspire you to walk the path of the Hearth Witch. While you may begin to learn how to work with natural resources from books like this one, the true teaching only comes when you start listening to the land and its plants and animals.

When the sacred within you recognises the sacred that surrounds you everywhere, a deeper spiritual reality opens up in which all space becomes sacred space, all time becomes sacred time, and all acts become sacred acts.

This is the true path of the Hearth Witch. Walk it in beauty.

Anna Franklin

THE
HEARTH
Witch's
PATH

Anna Franklin is a third-degree witch and high priestess of the Hearth of Arianrhod, and she has been a practicing Pagan for more than forty years. She is the author of over thirty books and the creator of the *Sacred Circle Tarot*, *Fairy Ring Oracle*, and the *Pagan Ways Tarot* (Schiffer, 2015). Her books have been translated into nine languages.

Anna has contributed hundreds of articles to Pagan magazines and has appeared on radio and TV. She lives and works in a village in the English Midlands, where she grows her own herbs, fruit, and vegetables, and generally lives the Pagan life. Visit her online at www.Anna Franklin.co.uk.

THE
HEARTH
Witch's
PATH

EVERYDAY RITUALS
AND SPELLS FOR
THE HOME

ANNA FRANKLIN

LLEWELLYN
WOODBURY, MINNESOTA

The Hearth Witch's Path: Everyday Rituals and Spells for the Home Copyright © 2025 by Anna Franklin. All rights reserved. No part of this book may be used or reproduced in any manner whatsoever, including internet usage, without written permission from Llewellyn Worldwide Ltd., except in the case of brief quotations embodied in critical articles and reviews. No part of this book may be used or reproduced in any manner for the purpose of training artificial intelligence technologies or systems.

FIRST EDITION
First Printing, 2025

Based on book design by Becky Zins
Cover design by Verlynda Pinckney
Interior floral background © Dover Publications
Interior floral woodcut © *1167 Decorative Cuts* (New York: Dover Publications, 2007)

Llewellyn is a registered trademark of Llewellyn Worldwide Ltd.

Library of Congress Cataloging-in-Publication Data (Pending)

ISBN 978-0-7387-7712-2

Llewellyn Worldwide Ltd. does not participate in, endorse, or have any authority or responsibility concerning private business transactions between our authors and the public.

All mail addressed to the author is forwarded but the publisher cannot, unless specifically instructed by the author, give out an address or phone number.

Any internet references contained in this work are current at publication time, but the publisher cannot guarantee that a specific location will continue to be maintained. Please refer to the publisher's website for links to authors' websites and other sources.

Llewellyn Publications
A Division of Llewellyn Worldwide Ltd.
2143 Wooddale Drive
Woodbury MN 55125-2989

WWW.LLEWELLYN.COM

Printed in the United States of America

Disclaimer

The information in this book is provided for educational and entertainment purposes only. It does not constitute a recommendation for use.

Contents

LIST OF RECIPES   XIII

INTRODUCTION   1

PART ONE
. . . .
Hearth and Home   3

Chapter 1: The Hearth…5

Chapter 2: The House Spirit…13

Chapter 3: The Witch's Kitchen and Home…21

Chapter 4: Magical Cleansing and Banishing…33

Chapter 5: Warding…41

PART TWO
. . . .
Herb Cunning   53

Chapter 6: Beginning to Work with Herbs…55

Chapter 7: The Hearth Witch's Garden…65

Chapter 8: Herbs in Magic…69

CONTENTS

Part Three

· · · · · · · · · ·

Working with the Gods   83

Chapter 9: Personal Practice…85

Chapter 10: Consecration…89

Chapter 11: Creating Sacred Space…95

Chapter 12: Ritual…103

Part Four

· · · · · · · · · ·

Natural Cycles   115

Chapter 13: The Cycle of the Year…117

Chapter 14: The Eight Sabbats…121

Chapter 15: Cycles of the Moon…155

Part Five

· · · · · · · · · ·

Operative Witchcraft   173

Chapter 16: Spells…177

Chapter 17: Spell Formulations…203

Chapter 18: Talismans and Amulets…213

Conclusion   217

Appendix 1: Elemental Correspondences   219

Appendix 2: Planetary Correspondences   223

Appendix 3: Metal Correspondences   231

CONTENTS

Appendix 4: Colour Correspondences 233

Appendix 5: Gemstone Correspondences 237

Appendix 6: Magical Herb Substitutions 245

Appendix 7: Magical Ingredients for Food 255

Appendix 8: Herbs for Home Warding 259

Appendix 9: Fumigation Herbs 265

Bibliography 267

Recipes

Banishing Incense...75

Consecration Incense...78

Consecration Oil...81

Crone Incense...77

Dark Moon Incense...77

Earth Mother Incense...78

Empowered Bathwater...28

Father Sun Incense...78

Full Moon Incense...76

Full Moon Oil...80

Hearth Goddess Incense...77

Herb Tea Basic Recipe...63

Herbal Shower Purification...28

Honouring the Goddess of the Stove...23

House Blessings Incense...74

House Cleansing Incense...75

House Spirit Incense...74

RECIPES

Love Incense...79

Lustral Water...34

Mooncakes...160

Peace and Harmony Rose Laundry Rinse...29

Potpourri for Domestic Harmony...30

Protection Oil...80

Protective Ivy Laundry Liquid...29

Purification Bath Salts...27

Relinquishing Oil...80

Rose Macerated Oil...81

Self-Blessing Oil...80

Violet Oil...81

Waning Moon Incense...76

Waning Moon Purification Bath...81

Waxing Moon Incense...75

Introduction

This volume explores the magical path of the hearth witch and how we form a spiritual relationship with the world. It is not a book of recipes and herbal how-tos, which I have covered extensively in other books in my Hearth Witch series. This is a book of magic.

. . . .

I've been a witch for all my adult life. I've worked with a coven for decades—a group of friends who meet to celebrate the sabbats and to learn from each other. With my experience, I'll help you answer this question: How does the individual witch build a spiritual relationship with the world and with the Gods on a day-to-day basis?

I coined the term "hearth witch" for my own approach to living the Craft as a daily spiritual path when I wrote my first book on the subject (*Hearth Witch*, Lear Books, 2003). I'm glad that both the term and path have resonated with so many around the world. I think it demonstrates a longing for a more centred, meaningful life and a sacred connection with our environment.

For decades, I have tried to live in harmony with the seasons, marking their changes, growing and working with our green kin, the plants, preserving food and honouring the bounty of Mother Earth, making jams, wines, meads and ales, incenses and potions. My personal practice begins at the centre of household life, the hearth, which in times past was the domestic altar, the place to communicate with the Gods and make offerings to protective household deities. When we begin at the centre, living consciously and with intent, our lives become infinitely richer, and we make deep connections with the sacred.

This knowledge is our heritage as women and as witches of all genders. For thousands of years, women amassed skills that were underacknowledged and seldom recorded, but most women possessed knowledge that was vital for survival, for nearly every woman had to know the mysteries of childbirth and how to provide meals, manage a home, grow her garden, keep her bees, and use herbs for healing, as well as the crafts of brewing, spinning, weaving, and dyeing; also, the local folklore and stories, divination, spells, and magical protections. Their magic was more intimately and more deeply connected to the tides of life than any ritual magician's. How easy it was for male authorities to condemn those women who knew a bit too much for their own good as witches, feared and cloaked in the garb of otherness. Yet they were the wise women who cared for the bodies and spirits of those around them, telling their fortunes, treating their bodily ailments with herbs, dowsing their lost property, physicking their farm animals—midwives who brought life into the world and laid out the dead at its end. They were the handywomen, blessers, herbwives, the cunning folk who got their hands dirty and showed up to do the hard and hallowed work.

The path of the hearth witch does not begin and end with recipes and sparkly little spells, but every day strives to form a sacred relationship with the world and the divine powers that underlie it, beginning with what is closest to us—not something mundane, but an environment woven through with magic and enchantment.

In this book, I hope to show you how.

Part One
Hearth and Home

A house is not just a shelter. On a physical and emotional level, it represents security and all we work for. It is probably where we spend most of our time, the place we share with our loved ones and where we invite our friends. Our homes are a reflection and extension of our inner selves—our tastes, our desires, and even our state of mind. The home is the centre of every family's world.

On a spiritual level, the home is much more. In magical practices and mythologies throughout the world, the home is a mystic connection to the flow of spiritual energies and the realms of the Gods. The Neolithic Celtic roundhouse, for example, with the fire at the centre, the square hearth, the smoke escaping through the thatched roof, was a representation of the cosmos—the walls of the hut were the circumference of the universe, the hearthstone the earth, its four sides the four directions and the four seasons, while the presence of the Gods was manifested in the living fire.[1]

In the past, weaving the subtle energies of the house with a network of symbols, shrines, and offerings ensured the prosperity and well-being of its inhabitants. How well a family created a relationship with its deities and the spirits of the land the home stood on determined their fortune.

This connection began at the doorway, the threshold between the home and the outside world. In ancient Rome this was protected by Mercury, the messenger god who had access to any realm, whose symbol was stroked when entering or leaving the

---

1 Michell, *At the Centre of the World.*

house for luck. In Greece, the *hekataion*, a shrine of the goddess Hekate, was placed at the threshold of the house to protect the home from evil.

Within the house, the Romans honoured the *lares familiares* (ancestral spirits) and the *lares domestici* (spirits of the home). Their shrine, the *lararium*, housed their images and was honoured daily with prayers and offerings. The *penates* guarded the larder and storeroom to ensure food was plentiful and kept well. In ancient Greece, *Zeus Ktesios* (Zeus of the Storeroom) guarded the prosperity of the home. He was represented in the storeroom by a two-handled pot filled with water, olive oil, and fruit, tightly stoppered and wrapped in white wool. The same ideas are reflected in most ancient societies, and the belief in such domestic gods survived until comparatively recent times (and in some places continues) in the form of household spirits or fairies, such as the British brownies and hobs, the Russian *domovoi*, and the Finnish *kotihaltia*. There are many, many more around the world.

The lesson is clear. It is in our homes that the first resonance of the sacred lies and where magic is at its most intimate. How we live there affects us physically, emotionally and, moreover, spiritually. The hearth was once the holy heart of the home, but what is its modern equivalent? The TV? The computer? And what effect does that have on our lives and our connection to the spiritual landscape?

As we have seen, in a magical sense, the domestic home is a mirror of the cosmos. The belief that control of the cosmos and entry to its various realms can be gained by re-creating it in miniature is an ancient one, exemplified by the old Hermetic maxim "as above, so below." According to Plato's Laws, the cosmic order is taken as the pattern for any temple or shrine. On the domestic scale, this begins with the hearth as sacred centre, which becomes a cosmic axis connecting this world and the realm of the Gods, its rising smoke taking prayers to the upperworld while the underworld of the dead and unborn, the seeds in the earth, reside beneath the hearthstone. Radiating out, the four walls of the house stand for the four directions and the four seasons. Conscious ritual movement through the house becomes movement through the cosmos.

CHAPTER 1

· · · · · · · · · · · · ·

The Hearth

The hearth fire has been the centre of human life for hundreds of thousands of years. In frozen blustery winter days, it meant the difference between survival and death, between comfort and cold pain. The hearth is the centre where we begin, the heart of the home where families gather to eat and cook, talk and warm themselves, and listen to stories. The hearth has been considered a sacred place since humans discovered fire.

Hearth Goddesses

Moreover, the domestic hearth fire is the dwelling place of the hearth goddess, who manifests in every flame. Every land has known her.

Traditionally, the woman of the house tended the hearth fire and acted as her household priestess. We seek to revive this tradition, to honour the hearth goddess, and to make the hearth an altar and shrine. Whenever I light a fire or candle, I do it with an invocation to her, to bring her presence into my home. By connecting with the energies of your hearth and its goddess, you invite ancient magic into your life.

Often, we simply call this deity the hearth goddess, though she has had many names.

HESTIA

In Greek myth, the hearth goddess is Hestia, whose name means "hearth" or, according to Plato, "the essence of things," a formless core symbolised by the flame, a pure essence that flows through everything that has life. She is the most peaceable of the Gods and never took part in their wars and arguments. She never married and refused a throne on Olympus to look after the hearth of the Gods, the still point at the centre of the cosmos. She is the calm centre, and the hearth is her altar and shrine, representing security and the solemn duty of hospitality. Her hearth was in the care of the woman of the house. Hestia presided over all hearth and altar fires and was worshipped daily with prayers before and after meals. Before each meal, a cake was thrown onto the fire as an offering to her.

SYMBOLS: fire, hearth, flames

OFFERINGS: incense, aromatic herbs, wheat or barley cakes, wine

INVOCATION

> *Hestia, daughter of Kronos, I call to you.*
> *You are the first and the last.*
> *You dwell in the flame of every hearth fire; you are the centre of the home.*
> *You tend the cosmic fire, the still dwelling place of the Gods.*
> *Smiling and gentle goddess, your way is peace and kindness.*
> *Accept these offerings and be with me [us]*
> *Look upon me [us] with benevolence*
> *Bring your gifts of compassion, good health, and goodness.*

VESTA

Vesta is the virgin fire goddess of Rome. Like Hestia, she refused a place in heaven, preferring to remain on earth, tending the fires in homes and temples. She was worshipped in private households, and each day, during a meal, a small cake was thrown on the fire for her; it was good luck if it burnt with a crackle. She was also worshipped in an important state cult maintained in a circular chamber housing the *ignis inextinctus* (undying fire), which was served by six chaste priestesses called the vestal virgins. Vesta's hearth symbolised the spirit and permanence of Rome itself.

SYMBOLS: hearth, sacred fire, the hollow fire stick used to light the sacred fire by rotation

OFFERINGS: wine, bread, cakes, food offerings, incense

INVOCATION

> *Vesta, virgin goddess of the undying fire,*
> *I call to you.*
> *Lady of the central fire, the focus of the home, accept my offerings.*
> *Bring your flame of divine love to my hearth and home.*
> *Come dwell here in friendship and hospitality, in kindness and compassion.*
> *Let me [us] feel your quiet strength.*

FRIGG

In Norse mythology, Frigg (beloved one) is the wife of Odin and queen of the Aesir. She is the goddess of the hearth, home, and domestic arts, as well as love, marriage, fertility, and childbearing. Such was her importance that only she, of all the Gods, could share Odin's high seat and look out over the universe.

SYMBOLS: spinning wheel, spindle, silver, mistletoe, mead horn

OFFERINGS: mead, milk, baked goods

INVOCATION

> *Hail, Frigg, queen of heaven*
> *Who sees all things, come to me [us].*
> *Goddess of the hearth and home*
> *Shelter and protect me [us];*
> *Bless this house and all within.*
> *Guide me [us] with your wisdom,*
> *To live with joy, love, and abundance*
> *With skill and strength.*
> *Come, Frigg; come and accept this offering I [we] make you.*

HABONDIA

Habondia is an Anglo-Saxon goddess of hearth and home honoured with fire. Her name means "the abundant one" and she is associated with plenty, prosperity, and the fruits of the harvest. She often appears in old texts presiding over witches' sabbats.

SYMBOLS: cornucopia, seeds, fruits, eggs, fire

OFFERINGS: fire, ale, beer, seeds, fruits, eggs

INVOCATION

Habondia, friend of witches, I call to you.

Come, accept this offering I make to you.

Lady of plenty, bless this house with good health and abundance.

Habondia, I honour you and ask for your gifts.

Blessed be.

BRIGHID

Brighid is a pan-Celtic goddess, appearing as Brighid or Brigit in Ireland, Brigantia in Northern England, Bride in Scotland, and Brigandu in Brittany. Her name is variously interpreted as meaning "fiery arrow," "the bright one," and "the powerful one" or "the high one." She is a triple goddess: the Brighid of poetry, prophecy, and inspiration who invented ogham; the Brighid of healing waters and midwifery; and the Brighid of fire who oversees the hearth and the forge and who is the patroness of craftspeople. She also has aspects as a goddess of fertility, livestock, and warfare.

Her festival was Imbolc (February 1), which marked the first stirrings of spring when young sheep were born and when ewes came into milk.

SYMBOLS: fire, Brighid's cross, Brighid doll

OFFERINGS: milk, candles, poetry, dandelions, swan feather, blackberries

INVOCATION

Brighid, daughter of the morning

Keeper of the sacred fire

I kindle this flame in your honour.

Come to me [us] and guide me [us]

Be a light in the darkness to me [us]

Let the fire of the hearth offer warmth and comfort

Let the fire of healing flow through me [us]

Let the flame of inspiration kindle my [our] creativity.

Come, Brighid, come; bless this hearth and home.

GABIJA

Gabija is the Lithuanian fire goddess, her name derived from the verb *apgaubti*, which means "to cover up" and refers to the practice of the mistress of the house banking the fire at night so that it will neither go out nor spread from the hearth. Care was taken not to offend the goddess. The fire could only be extinguished with cold clean water and people were not allowed to spit into it. When it was being lit, everyone had to remain silent.

She was attended only by women, particularly the head woman of the clan or house. She was invoked at all family rituals and occasions. She was also a mediator, carrying prayers to the other Gods. She had special festivals at the beginning of February dedicated to the renewal of the hearth fire and the household Gods. An eternal flame once burned at Sventaragis Valley tended by priestesses known as *vaidilutės*.

SYMBOLS: fire, the colour red, cat

OFFERINGS: bread, salt, water

INVOCATION

> *Gabija, fiery one, I call to you*
> *I kindle this flame in your honour* [light a candle or fire]
> *I offer you this salt so you might be nourished*
> *I offer you this water so that you may bathe and rest,*
> *Come bless my* [our] *hearth and home.*

Charge of the Hearth Goddesses

Listen to the words of the hearth goddess, who of old was called amongst men Hestia, Vesta, Frigg, Habondia, Brighid, and Gabija, among many other names. I am the bright one, the fiery one, the formless one, the living flame of spirit that flows throughout the cosmos. I am the first and the last.

Worship me with fire, for I am the divine spark of creation, the goddess who dwells in every flame. I am the glow in the hearth, the fire in your heart, and the spark of inspiration in your mind.

I am the gentlest of all the Gods. I am the calm centre. All acts of hospitality, compassion, love, joy, and friendship are my rituals.

I am the keeper of the eternal flame. I tend the still hearth of the Gods, about which the cosmos spins. As it is above, so it is below; all hearths are my shrines, all keepers of the hearth are my priests and priestesses. Honour me there, and I will teach you the ancient magic that only love may know.

The Hearth as a Cosmic Axis

As the dwelling place of the living goddess, the hearth is a holy place, a sacred centre, where the living presence of the goddess manifests—a threshold between this world and the realm of the Gods. Its rising smoke takes prayers to the Gods of the upperworld, while the Gods of the worlds below can be contacted through the hearthstone.

Working with Your Hearth

If you are lucky enough to have an open fire, your hearth is ready, and you can begin to work with it. However, don't worry if you don't have one. Many people just have an electric stove in the kitchen and central heating in the living room. This doesn't matter; remember that the hearth is a symbol for the hospitality and living spirit of the home. The hearth goddess is present in any living flame, so you can choose a suitable place to be the centre of your practice—a mantlepiece, altar, or your kitchen—and set up your shrine of the hearth goddess, the centre from which all else radiates. The important thing is to have a living flame of some sort, such as a candle or an oil lamp.

Invocation to Light an Open Fire

When you make up the fire and prepare to light it, do so with these words:

> *Hearth goddess*
> *You, who tends the hearth of the Gods, keeper of the eternal flame*
> *Hearth goddess, in this act I honour you.*
> *Draw near and bestow grace and blessing upon my home.*
> *Let peace, love, and grace dwell here.*

Using the Mantlepiece as Your Hearth

You may not have an open fire but rather a mantlepiece over a gas or electric fire. This is ideal to place candles or lamps to house the living flame of the goddess. You might also have a small statue or representation of the hearth goddess there.

Using a Hearth Goddess Altar

Instead of an open fire or mantelpiece, you might set up a small altar for the hearth goddess. Use a candle as the living flame, and perhaps include a statuette of a hearth goddess such as Vesta or Brighid. You can also place offerings of flowers and food on the altar.

Using the Kitchen as Your Hearth

The stove has taken the place of the hearth fire as the means of cooking and preparing meals, and the kitchen is often the place where everyone gathers and spends family time, just as the central hearth of older homes once was. You might want to use your kitchen, a place near your stove, or even your stove itself as your hearth. Remember that you will need a living flame to embody the goddess, so you can set up a tray with a candle and offerings on it.

Using Candles

Choose a suitable candle, perhaps a large, long-burning one that may be lit day after day.

Consecrate the candle with consecration oil (page 81) from the centre to the top and then from the centre to the bottom while saying these words:

> *I consecrate this candle and set it aside to house the living presence of the hearth goddess. With this oil, I consecrate it. With these words, I consecrate it. Consecrated, blessed be.*

Light the candle with these words:

> *Hearth goddess*
> *I kindle this flame to honour you.*
> *It is your living presence*
> *Let it burn within me*
> *In peace, in love*
> *May all within this home know your blessing.*

If it is a large candle, you can put it out when you wish to and relight it again with the same invocation of the goddess (you don't need to reconsecrate it every time).

Taking a Hearth Goddess Candle to a New Home

When moving to a new house, it was often the custom to take live coals from the previous hearth to ensure the continuation of the life and spirit of the home and family. You can repeat a similar custom by lighting a candle brought from your old home in the new one. This echoes the carrying of Hestia's sacred fire to new colonies and towns.

• • • • •

CHAPTER 2

. . . .

The House Spirit

In traditional pagan societies, the spirits of the household are acknowledged and venerated. They are the protective spirits of a house who safeguard its happiness and prosperity, and look after the family. The Romans called such a spirit the *lar familiaris* and gave it daily offerings of food and monthly gifts of garlands, all placed on the hearth shrine, and it was always invoked on special occasions such as birthdays, weddings, births, and deaths.

In addition to a central shrine to Vesta, most Roman families maintained shrines for a panoply of small domestic Gods: the lares, protectors of the household; and the penates, Gods of pantry and larder. Shrines to the lares and penates were located conveniently close to the door so that offerings could be made frequently—for, like the house fairies of British and Irish lore, they were troublesome if neglected. The door itself was watched over by Janus, the two-faced god of doors and gates associated with endings and beginnings. He was joined in his duties by Cardea, the goddess of door handles and hinges. Ovid tells us that Cardea's power is "to open what is shut, and to shut what is open." As a result, she was also the goddess of midwives, called upon during difficult childbirths. The threshold, and the act of crossing over it, belonged to the trickster god Mercury (Hermes in Greek), whose sign, a phallic stone or statue, often stood guard at the front of the dwelling. It was customary to stroke the stone for luck when leaving or returning home.

Such legends persisted in different forms into recent times. The brownie, known in Scotland and the north of England, was a solitary house fairy who became attached to particular houses or families and who did odd jobs about the house and farm, cleaning, tidying up, or helping with the brewing. The only reward he asked for was a bowl of cream left by the hearth. In the Shetland Isles in the early eighteenth century, every family of substance had a brownie to whom they made offerings. When the milk was churned, a few drops were sprinkled in every corner of the house for him. When they brewed ale, a few drops were sprinkled into the hole in the brownie's stone. There was also a special stack or corn called the brownie's stack, which was never fenced or roped like the others, but which no wind ever seemed to blow away. In Russia, the *domovoi* (house spirit) looks after a house and its residents. It lives behind the oven or beneath the threshold. When a family moves into a new house, they should put a slice of bread under the stove to attract a *domovoi*, since the prosperity of the household depends on him. Once one is in residence, it will do various chores around the house as long as food is left out for it every night. When moving house, the oldest woman had to take a coal from the old house to kindle a fire in the new home. When she arrived, she would strike the doorposts and ask, "Grandfather, are visitors welcome?" while the master and mistress welcomed the fairy to the new dwelling and offered him bread and salt.

It doesn't matter whether you really believe that a little man lives behind the stove; thinking of your home as a living spirit that needs to be nurtured shifts your focus on how you live within it. Every house has its own spirit, what we detect as an atmosphere when we enter it. I remember when I and a group of other witches rented a holiday cottage for a spiritual retreat. The place had been unsympathetically renovated and seemed atmospherically and spiritually dead when we arrived. We started to make offerings to the house spirit, shared food from each meal, lit candles and spoke to it. Within two days, the house woke up and started to take notice, and we were warmly welcomed in, and the withdrawn house began to enjoy having us there and became positively cheerful.

Household Gods Shrine

For the ancients, the hearth was also the altar of the household gods where offerings could be made, such as a fragment of food from a meal or garlands on special family occasions such as birthdays and weddings. You might use your mantelpiece as an altar set with images that represent your household spirit(s) and an offering dish in which you can place morsels of food or flowers. Dedicate it by lighting a white candle and say,

House spirit, I make you this place, which I will keep sacred.
I honour you and will treat your dwelling place with love.
I will treat this house with care in your honour.
I make you this offering and ask for your protection from harm.

Make an offering of some bread and rosemary in the offering bowl. On a regular basis, make an offering of food or drink and thank the spirit—don't just do it when you want something! This can later be burned on the fire or put out for the birds.

Kitchen Spirit Altar

If you don't have a fireplace and a traditional hearth, the kitchen is an ideal place for an altar that honours the household spirit. You can set up an altar on a shelf, in a kitchen niche, privately in a cupboard, or on a tray on the countertop. Place on it an image that represents the house spirit or something that you associate with the sanctity and work of the home, candles, and a bowl for offerings.

Spirit Houses

Instead of a house spirit altar, you might like to have a spirit house. These are small pottery or wooden houses that are ceremonially offered to the household spirit as a dwelling place. A friend told me that he places his spirit house on the stairs, the midpoint between up and down, and in the last fourteen years it has moved through four houses with him, and each time when he moves in, he does a ritual to honour the spirit of the new house and invites it to take up residence in the spirit house. When he moves out of a house, he does a ritual thanking the spirit for his home, protection, and love and asking for the spirit house to be given back to him so it can move to its new location. It is the first thing to enter his new home and the last thing to leave.

Ritual to Invite the Household Spirit into a Spirit House

You will need the following items to conduct this ritual:

Spirit house, made or bought

House spirit incense (page 74)

Small white candle

Food offering made from grain (e.g., bread)

Light the candle and try to sense the house spirit, the personality of the house, around you. Make an offering of incense before the spirit house and place the food offering inside it, saying,

House spirit, I make you this place
And invite you to dwell within it.
I honour you and will treat your dwelling place with love.
I make you this offering and ask for your protection from harm.

Make sure you keep the spirit house clean and make regular offerings of food to it. After twenty-four hours, empty the spirit house and put the food out for the birds.

Ritual of Greeting the Household Spirit in a New Home

You will need the following items for this ritual:

Bread

Salt

Small pretty plate or offering bowl

Small white candle

House spirit incense (page 74)

The first thing you should do in a new home is greet its house spirit, offering it bread and salt. If you haven't done it before, make time to do it now. Go to your hearth (or kitchen stove) and try to be aware of the house spirit's presence. Light the candle and incense. Say,

House spirit, I greet you.
Know that I will honour you and treat you with respect.
I offer you this incense.
I offer you this bread, symbol of nourishment [put the bread on the plate]
I offer you this salt, symbol of hospitality [put the salt on the plate]

House spirit, I greet you.
Know me and my intent
I ask you to protect this house.

You can then go on to make the hearth spirit shrine or invite the spirit into the spirit house.

~~~~~~

Reconnect with an Alienated House Spirit

Usually, if you start to talk regularly to your house spirit and make frequent offerings, it will be enough to win it around. If you feel that the house spirit has become so alienated it has left, go out into the garden wearing your best clothes, taking with you bread and salt. Bow to the east, to the south, to the west, and to the north. Say,

House spirit, forgive us and return to us, for we need your care.

Go indoors and put the salted bread, wrapped in a white cloth, inside the house near the front door and say,

House spirit, come live with us and tend our home.

~~~~~~

Offerings to the Household Spirits

It is traditional to offer the household spirit a few drops of milk, bread, or honey, especially at family gatherings and occasions. These represent one given food, one formed, and one found. If they are plentiful, they indicate that all is well with the land and it is productive. You might not want to offer some of these particular foods and substitutions can be made. Some of my Scottish friends say whisky is very effective!

This domestic ritual will help you bring spiritual practice into your daily life and sacredness into your home. Offer a tiny portion of each meal with these words:

House spirit, I honour you.
This food is the work of many hands
And I offer you a share.
House spirit, accept my gift
And upon my hearth, leave your blessings.

Put this food out for the birds the next day. On special occasions, honour your house spirit with flowers on the hearth or shrine.

Honouring the Household Spirits

If you think of cleaning and tidying as honouring the household spirits, not only does this make the task more pleasant, but it brings you into a new relationship with your home.

Threshold Shrine

The threshold is a liminal place. It lies between the inside and outside, belonging to neither. This meant it was surrounded by a variety of rituals and taboos. In many places, it should never be trodden on, but carefully stepped over. The Finns and Germans often made the sills high to make sure this happened. In Russia, men would always cross themselves when crossing a threshold. When you cross someone's threshold, you enter their personal space, and by the laws of hospitality are under their protection and their guardian deities and owe them the duties of a good guest in return.

The sanctity of the threshold was protected with images of protective spirits and amulets, or gold coins for luck, buried beneath it or protective symbols drawn upon it. Offerings were placed on the threshold.

You might like to have a shrine to protective deities (such as Hekate, Hermes, or Mercury or a deity from your tradition) on your threshold, in your porch, or by the front door. Make regular offerings of flowers and grain upon it.

HOUSE BLESSING RITUAL

To begin working with your home as your personal temple, you might like to perform a house blessing ritual. Go to your hearth or altar. Light a house blessings incense (page 74) and a white candle and say,

> Lord and Lady, bless this home
> Bless each wall and bless each stone.
> Bless this home from roof to floor
> Bless each window and each door.
> Bless each room and bless each wall

Bless the hearth and bless the hall.
Bless the table and bless the bread
Bless the stove and bless the bed.
Bless all who live here, kith and kin
Bless friends who enter, welcomed in.
From below and from above
Be a place of peace and love.
Surround it now with your protection
Above, below, and in each direction.
Lord and Lady, blessed be.

CHAPTER 3

. . . .

The Witch's Kitchen and Home

We often think of the kitchen as the heart of the home, the place where we gather to cook, eat, and share with friends. You might even think of your stove as the sacred centre of your home, your hearth. The kitchen is probably also the place where we make our magical foods and brews, tinctures and salves, and perhaps cast our spells.

Even if you don't, the everyday kitchen is a magical workshop, the oven an alchemical tool that transmutes raw ingredients into sustenance for the body and spirit. Food is life, a gift of Mother Earth, and we acknowledge that gift only when we treat it with reverence. Preparing, cooking, and serving food is a day-to-day ritual of hospitality, love, and sharing that expresses the cycle of the year when fresh seasonal food is used. Whether you are cooking for a sabbat or just for supper, treat it as a conscious act of magic and reflect that when you eat, you take in the life energy of the food you are consuming, not just its nutrition.

Prepare your food with intent. Do not cook when you are angry as the energy transfers into the food. Use your wooden spoon as a magic wand, adding blessings as you stir. Stir your dishes sunwise to wind up the magic. Inscribe your kitchen tools with magical sigils (invisibly with water if you wish). Add ingredients to food for their magical properties. Eat seasonal food to harmonise with the cycles of nature. Eat consciously. Give thanks to Mother Earth for her gifts.

. . . . .

Adding Magical Ingredients to Food

Each ingredient possesses its own virtues and energies, and you can utilise these gifts to create culinary magic. You can cook up a love feast, a meal for peace and healing, or a dish of abundance. Adding healing herbs and spices to food is one way we can care for ourselves. (See appendix 7.)

SEASONAL FOOD

Our ancestors were deeply connected to the cycle of the seasons. They knew what grew when and where. They depended on the harvest to survive. Summer might have been a time of plenty, but in winter, unless sufficient stores had been laid by, they would starve. Now we can buy any food all year round from the shops and goods are imported from thousands of miles away; many have lost sight of the natural cycles. To reconnect with the wheel of the year, you can try eating seasonal and local food and even growing some of your own, if you have the space. Do some research into what seasonal dishes our ancestors ate and introduce them into your seasonal celebrations.

RITUAL FOOD

The pagan festivals of the year, including the eight sabbats, are based on the annual round of sowing, nurturing, harvesting, and winter rest. It was the great central theme of ancient religion.

When we incorporate food into a ritual, such as when we share bread and wine, it represents both physical nourishment and spiritual sustenance. We recognise the god essence, the spiritual core within the food we consume, and eat it consciously to sustain us. The sharing of food, particularly bread and wine, was part of many ancient pagan religions long before the advent of Christianity.

Ritual food should connect us to the cycle of the year, with seasonal ingredients and dishes. Festival bread should be made by hand with a blessing. You can add fresh herbs, nuts, and berries to your bread at different times of the year. I like to make country wines from seasonal flowers, fruits, and vegetables. At Beltane I make wine from hawthorn flowers, and this is ready to drink the next year at Beltane, linking one cycle to the next, for example. At Midsummer, I might make strawberry wine or an herbal mead (called a metheglin), and so on.

FOOD OFFERINGS AND LIBATIONS

If the food has been made with intent and consecration, it becomes more than ordinary food, and thus makes a suitable offering to the Gods and spirits. After we bless the bread and wine, before we take any, we offer a portion to the Gods. Bread is thrown onto the fire so that its essence might be released to them with the words "the first is always for the Gods." A libation of wine is made in a similar manner. (A libation is a pouring of wine, milk, or other drink onto the ground or before an image as an offering to the Gods.) We always leave more food behind in the woods or garden for the local spirits after the feast. In reality, of course, it is the animals and birds that eat it, but we consider that first the spirits consume its essence.

THE STOVE

The Slavs viewed the hearth or stove as a sacred space with a feminine aspect referred to as mother or provider. Indeed, in many cultures, the oven is seen as a kind of womb that opens and gives birth to the bread within. In Britain, we still talk of someone being pregnant as "having a bun in the oven." In Russia, midwives would even "re-bake" sickly children in the (cool) oven to give them a second birth.

The Romans worshipped Fornax (furnace), the goddess of the oven who oversaw the proper baking of bread and also had links to fertility. Her festival, the *Fornacalia*, was around February 17. Ovens were decorated with garlands and spelt grains were communally toasted in the local meeting hall, as well as special loaves of bread.

HONOURING THE GODDESS OF THE STOVE

To honour the mother of the stove or your own hearth goddess, consider cleaning your oven as a sacred act. You will need the following:

BICARBONATE OF SODA (BAKING SODA)

1 CUP WHITE VINEGAR

3 CUPS WATER

Mix the water and vinegar. Put into a spritzer bottle. Bless it with these words:

Mother of the oven
Witness that I consecrate this potion
That it may cleanse and bless
As I honour you, mother of the oven
Consecrated, blessed be.

Sprinkle the oven with baking soda and spray with your liquid. It will fizz. Leave for thirty minutes. Wipe off, then wash off with clean water.

Afterward, make some bread and put it to bake in the oven with these words:

> *Hearth goddess, goddess of the oven, lady of fire, you are a goddess of transformation, taking raw ingredients and transmuting them into nourishing food. On this day I honour you and bake this bread in tribute.*

Share the bread with friends and be sure to put the crumbs out for the wild birds.

PLANTS TO KEEP IN THE KITCHEN

Many people keep a few pots of growing herbs or flowers on their kitchen windowsill. Some plants have energies that will benefit the home and its inhabitants:

Basil

Growing a basil plant in the kitchen brings a sacred energy to your home; in Hinduism, holy basil is the mother goddess incarnated in plant form, a protective spirit that deflects negative energy from its surroundings, bringing peace, prosperity, and blessing.

Aloe Vera

Keep a plant in your kitchen for protection. Aloe leaves are a good remedy for accidental burns in the kitchen—simply split a leaf and spread the gel from the middle of it on the affected area.

Geranium (Pelargonium), Scented

Keep a plant in your kitchen for happiness, health, and prosperity.

Mint

Mint is a protective herb that keeps out flies.

The Witch's Stillroom

Once, many homes had a stillroom, so called because it usually contained a still for distilling flower essences for perfume and medicinal purposes. It was a separate place from the general kitchen and was kept clean and sweet smelling with drying herbs and flowers. In it, the woman of the house made her herbal infusions, salves, oils, compresses, and poultices, her inks, dyes, soaps, household cleaners, and perfumes. Here, too, she brewed wine and ale, preserved fruit, and made jams and jellies, pickles and chutneys. She kept it locked and kept careful records of her recipes and experiments in her household book, which she had probably inherited from her own mother, recording all the family's formulas and herbal cures.

I love my own stillroom (actually the utility room), which is lined with fermenting homemade wine, drying herbs, bottles of herb oils and tinctures, jars of herbal salves, and all my homemade preserves. My small still stands on a shelf and my jam pan hangs from the ceiling. The freezer houses produce from the vegetable garden to keep us supplied during winter.

The Witch's Dining Room

We gather in the dining room (or around the kitchen table) to eat, to share, to connect and exchange stories with family and friends. If we make eating a conscious act, it reminds us of its spiritual connection to life and the bounty of Mother Earth. In some cultures, the dining table is a sacred space, the giving hand of the Gods, so it was unlucky for empty bottles or bowls to be left on it, and it was reserved only for eating and never used for other tasks.

Consider the magic you might bring to dining with different coloured candles and seasonal flowers to remind you of the wheel of the year—sunflowers for joy, begonias for friendship, calendula, carnations or roses for love, fuchsias for blessings, pelargoniums for happiness, and so on.

INVITING THE GODS

Some people like to set an extra place at the table and invite the Gods to join them at mealtimes. Do this with these words:

> *Noble Gods, I set a place at my table for you.*
> *I ask you to join me [us] here tonight.*
> *You are always welcome here*
> *In my home and at my hearth.*
> *Noble Gods, I honour you.*

FOOD BLESSING

When we eat, we should pause and thank Mother Earth who bears the harvest. Farmers, harvesters, truckers, shopworkers, and warehouse staff all play their part in getting our food to us. Animals and plants die so that we can live, and we should honour their sacrifice. Whatever we eat, it is the work of many. You can use this prayer as a simple blessing:

> *Mother Earth, you have given us your bounty.*
> *Father Sun, you have given us life.*
> *We give thanks to all who have made this meal possible.*
> *Lord and Lady, bless us as we eat.*

The Witch's Bedroom

At the end of the day, we retreat to the sanctuary of our bedrooms to sleep and dream, relax, meditate, or make love. It should be the place where we feel safest and most relaxed. It is the place of dreaming magic.

BEDROOM ALTAR

I choose to have an altar over the fireplace in my bedroom. It houses images of the God and Goddess, a Himalayan salt lamp and candles, seasonal flowers and decorations, and sometimes spells I am working on.

MORNING RITUAL

Start each day by setting positive intentions:

> *Father Sun, I greet you.*
> *Mother Earth, I thank you*
> *For the miracle of being alive*
> *In this beautiful world.*
> *I begin this day with hope.*
> *I begin this day with joy*
> *I begin this day with love.*

NIGHTLY RITUAL

It is good to have a daily ritual of gratitude to acknowledge simple blessings. Going to bed with good and loving thoughts contributes to a better sleep. At the end of the day, light a tealight (in a safe jar) on your bedroom altar. Say,

Lord and Lady, I greet you and honour you at the end of this day.

Thank them for all the good things the day has brought. Try to think of at least three: on good days, it might be wonderful new experiences and insights; on bad days, it might just be a good cup of coffee or a call from a friend. Say these out loud and finish with,

Lord and Lady, thank you for all your blessings.

The Witch's Bathroom

The bathroom is a place of cleansing and purification. If the hearth is where you connect with the element and deities of fire, the bathroom is where you can connect with the element and deities of water.

BATHROOM ALTAR

You don't have to have an altar in every room, but if you are trying to work with the energies of water, having an altar in the bathroom can be helpful. This can be a simple collection of seashells, blue candles, river pebbles, and so on placed on the windowsill. You could add statues of water deities, sea creatures, or mermaids.

RITUAL PURIFICATION

As you take your bath or shower, you may view it as a ritual purification, as well as a physical one. Visualise all negativity and illness leaving your body and dissolving into the water. As you pull the plug or watch the shower water go down the drain, visualise the negativity being returned to the earth, leaving you cleansed and renewed.

PURIFICATION BATH SALTS

4 TABLESPOONS SALT (CLEANSES AND PURIFIES)

FEW DROPS ROSEMARY OIL (CLEANSES AND PURIFIES)

FEW DROPS FRANKINCENSE OIL (CLEANSES, PURIFIES, AND RAISES VIBRATIONS)

Blend and store in an airtight container.

Use a handful in your bath as a ritual cleansing.

Herbal Shower Purification

HANDFUL FRESH MINT LEAVES (PURIFICATION)

HANDFUL FRESH ROSEMARY LEAVES (CLEANSING)

1 TABLESPOON JUNIPER BERRIES, CRUSHED (DISPELS NEGATIVITY)

1 TEASPOON FRESH GINGER, GRATED (PROTECTION, ENERGISING)

GRATED ZEST OF ONE GRAPEFRUIT (DETOXIFYING)

1 CUP SUNFLOWER OIL (BLESSINGS)

1½ CUPS SEA SALT (PURIFICATION)

5 TEASPOONS VITAMIN C POWDER

Put the mint, rosemary, juniper berries, ginger, and zest into a pan with the sunflower oil. Simmer on a low heat for five minutes. Strain, discarding the pulp and retaining the oil. In another bowl, combine the sea salt and vitamin C powder. Add the herb oil, mix well, and store in an airtight jar. This will keep for about six months. Use as a body scrub in the shower, rubbing onto wet skin and then rinsing well. Follow with a moisturiser.

Empowered Bathwater

You can empower your bathwater with intent. Water is the most receptive of all the elements, which is why it is connected with the emotions.

Take a clean glass jar. Paste on the outside of it (so that the word reads inward toward the contents of the jar) paper on which the word *love* has been written. Fill it with water. Leave overnight under a waxing or full moon. Add this to your bath and absorb the quality of love and acknowledge your worthiness of love.

The Witch's Laundry

Like the bathroom, the laundry is associated with the element of water and with cleansing. Rather than seeing the laundry as a chore, we can greet it as an opportunity to apply our magical and herbal knowledge to the task, to purify our clothes and imbue them with magical protection.

PEACE AND HARMONY ROSE LAUNDRY RINSE

4 CUPS ROSE WATER (LOVE, PEACE, AND BEAUTY)

½ TABLESPOON FRESH LAVENDER FLOWERS (HARMONY)

½ TABLESPOON ORRIS ROOT (PROTECTION)

2 DROPS CLOVE OIL (PROSPERITY)

Place in a large glass jar and leave on a sunny windowsill for fourteen days. Strain and add a teaspoonful to the final rinse water of your clothes.

PROTECTIVE IVY LAUNDRY LIQUID

Put a few handfuls of chopped English ivy (*Helix hedera*) leaves for protection in a large pan and cover with water. Simmer, with the lid on, for twenty to twenty-five minutes. Strain off the liquid. You can use this for hand-washing clothes or simply add a cupful to your washing machine. Ivy contains saponins (soap) and will make a good job of washing your clothes without the nasty chemicals of washing powder. Do not wash your dishes with this as, if ingested, ivy is slightly toxic and may upset your stomach.

The Witch's Living Room

The living room is where we gather, relax, and socialise with family and friends. It should be made as warm and welcoming as possible, with comfortable seating and cushions, relaxing colours, and sympathetic lighting. In the evening, candles create a calm atmosphere, and you can use coloured candles for different purposes. Scents should come from natural sources in the form of essential oil evaporators or potpourri: avoid chemical scents and sprays.

Living Room Altar

If you want to create a living room altar, you could use a small table or box covered with a cloth. Have on the altar images of gods that represent fellowship and family harmony, such as the Three Graces or the goddess Concordia. You could also place family and ancestor pictures on it. Use it as the place to perform ceremonies of family love and harmony.

. . . .

Potpourri for Domestic Harmony

Scented geranium, leaves and flowers (love, happiness, prosperity)

Lavender (peace and harmony)

Basil leaves (protection and luck)

Begonia flowers (friendship)

Passionflowers (peace and harmony)

Cardamom pods (friendship and joy)

Rose petals (love)

Orris root powder (protection)

Dry your flowers on paper for a few days. Mix the ingredients and seal together in a large jar for at least one month before using. Place in your living room to calm problems and bring peace and harmony.

Living Plant Allies

Keep a live plant in a pot in your living room.

African violet: protection, enhanced spirituality

Begonia: harmony

Calendula: protection, love

Carnation: love, protection

Chrysanthemum: ancestor connection, protection, cheerfulness

Crocus: friendship, love, peace

DAFFODIL: love, luck, fertility

FERN: home protection

FUCHSIA: love, blessing

GERANIUM: love, blessing, prosperity

JASMINE: love, beauty

LAVENDER: love

LILY: love, harmony

MINIATURE ROSE: love, peace

The Witch's Pantry

The pantry is an important place in the spiritual well-being and symbolic prosperity of the house. It is where we store all the foods we grow and buy, the fruits of our labours, whether through physical work in the garden or farm or through earning money to spend at the grocery store. We should respect this by ensuring the storeroom is kept clean and well organised and asking the protective gods of the house to keep the goods safe. In the ancient world, there were special gods and protective spirits of the storeroom. Once a year, when the harvest from the garden is gathered in, I pour a libation of wine to the gods of the pantry and ask for their protection:

> *Gods of the storeroom*
> *I greet you and honour you.*
> *Protect the bounty in your care.*
> *Bless this house with prosperity*
> *May there always be enough.*
> *Gods of the storeroom, blessed be.*

· · · · · · · · · · · · ·

Magical Cleansing and Banishing

As well as a physical cleansing, houses occasionally need a spiritual cleansing. You might be aware of the atmosphere of houses you visit, but unaware of the energy of your own home—you get used to it, just as you get used to domestic smells like dog odour, and stop being able to detect them. One of my old teachers used to say that houses can become "mazy," meaning that they had amassed an unpleasant or depleting spiritual miasma. A home can accumulate maziness from its history and environment and from prolonged emotional turmoil or conflict within its walls.

A spiritual miasma in your home may unwittingly be created by your own magical practices. I often read that magic is a neutral force that can be used for good or ill, and yes, that is true, but once we begin to shape it and direct it, it *becomes* anger, hate, love, healing, and that's the whole point of casting a spell or performing a ritual. If it stayed neutral it would be useless to us. If you have been dabbling in unethical magic, you may find it has a corrupting effect on you and your environment or find yourself the subject of unwanted and unpleasant attention by the low-level spirits that are attracted to it. If you have been firing off magic in an unconsidered and chaotic way, your home (and you) will need a thorough spiritual purification. We always do a spiritual cleansing before setting protection wards.

Personal Purification

The first thing is to cleanse ourselves of our own personal spiritual maziness. We should always do this before any kind of ritual, as we should not approach the Gods in an impure state, but it is doubly important if you are going to attempt a house cleansing or banishing. It is necessary to get rid of your own spiritual dirt before even attempting to clean your home; a part of the problem might be your own spiritual miasma affecting the dwelling. Take the following steps:

Take a purification bath or shower

Perform a ritual fumigation of your aura (page 35)

Consciously let go of anger, resentment, and so on, visualising them draining away from your body into the floor

Sprinkle yourself with lustral water

LUSTRAL WATER

Lustral is from the Latin *lustralis* and means "purification." Lustral water is a combination of the purifying energies of spring water and salt, consecrated and empowered.

Pour a cup of spring water. Say,

> *I charge and bless thee, creature of water, in the name of the Goddess.*

Measure a teaspoon of salt (any kind) and say,

> *I charge and bless thee, creature of salt, in the name of the Goddess.*

Add the salt to the water and stir three times with your forefinger. Say,

> *I charge and consecrate thee, in the name of the Goddess, that you may bless and purify all things you touch. So mote it be.*

RITUAL HOUSE CLEANING

This ritual should be carried out at the waning moon. All rituals for spiritually cleansing your house of negativity begin with a physical cleaning and tidying. It is important to move everything, as neglected corners and piles of possessions can accumulate stagnant energy.

Using a branch of hyssop or rosemary; sprinkle lustral water (see above) throughout the house, from top to bottom.

Use a purification wash (page 34) on all safe surfaces (not wood), saying as you use it,

> Be purified and cleansed. Be purified and cleansed. Be purified and cleansed.

You are then ready to perform your ritual fumigation or banishing.

Ritual Fumigation

If you feel that your home has accumulated negative energy, or if there is a bad atmosphere lingering after an argument, it may be possible to clear it with a simple smoke fumigation. The practice of burning herbs to cleanse and purify a place is common throughout the world. Various herbs have been used: for example, some Native American tribes use white sage, the Scots commonly "sained" with juniper, and the ancient Egyptians and Hebrews used frankincense. Don't just buy white sage; it is culturally significant and endangered. There are many other herbs that are effective for ritual cleansing and purification (page 265).

Open all the doors and windows. Use a smoking herb bundle (sain) or carry burning herbs or a blended incense of several herbs on charcoal (very carefully on a heatproof dish) as you walk from room to room, starting at the top of the house and working to the bottom, making sure you go into all the corners.

HOUSE CLEANSING RITUAL

If a simple ritual fumigation or lustration is not enough to clear your house, you might need to perform a house cleansing ritual. It is a good idea to do a house cleansing ritual on a regular basis at the waning moon, particularly if you work magically.

Give your house a thorough cleaning and tidying.

Use a ritual house purification wash (page 34) on all safe surfaces. Fumigate other surfaces with incense or herb smoke.

Open the back door. Sweep through the house from top to bottom, finishing at the back door, with a bundle of birch twigs (purification and new beginnings) or rowan twigs (banishing) or heather twigs (clears negativity), saying,

> I *sweep out all ill. I sweep out all ill. I sweep out all ill.*

(Keep repeating.) Finish by ejecting the negativity from the back door with a final flourish of your besom.

Open all the doors and windows to let out what you wish to be gone.

Carry a bowl of the house cleansing incense (page 75) from the top floor to the bottom, including all rooms and cupboards, finishing at the back door. Allow the smoke to go in each corner and say,

> I *cleanse this place*
> I *command all negativity to be gone.*
> *This do I will. So mote it be.*

Close the doors and windows. Light a white candle on your altar or hearth and say,

> *Lord and Lady*
> *Grant me your blessings*
> *As I give you my thanks and my service.*
> *Blessed be.*

You are now ready to set your protective wards.

BANISHING RITUAL

A house cleansing ritual is usually enough to remove an accumulated maziness from your home, but sometimes you may need to perform a banishing too. A banishing will leave a place energetically sterile, so be sure this is what you want. Be clear what your intent is. If you feel your house is haunted and has mischievous spirits, unless they are causing serious issues, it is best to leave such beings alone. If your banishing doesn't work, you might just make them mad! If you buy a house where something violent or foul has happened and you feel it still making the atmosphere ominous or unpleasant, then banishing may be warranted.

Banishing should not be undertaken lightly and should only be done when absolutely necessary. It shouldn't be repeated often, unlike cleansing. Banishing employs fumigation with banishing herbs, salt, sound, and ritual.

Begin by thoroughly cleaning and tidying the house. Use the ritual purification wash (page 34) on all suitable surfaces. Take a purification bath (page 81).

Perform this ritual during the dark moon. You will need the following:

WHITE ALTAR CLOTH

ASPERGER (BUNCH OF PURIFICATION HERBS SUCH AS ROSEMARY AND SAGE USED TO SPRINKLE)

NEW WHITE CANDLE IN A HOLDER

MATCHES

BOWL OF WATER

BOWL OF SALT

BANISHING INCENSE OR BANISHING HERB SMOKE

BELL

PROTECTION OIL (PAGE 80)

TRAY

Lay a clean white cloth on your altar. Lay out the tools you will need. Have clear in your mind what you want to banish. Open all the windows and doors.

Go to the hearth and say,

> *Hearth goddess, you are the still centre, the living flame. Hearth goddess, nurturer, protector, be with me and aid my rite as I banish all evil and negativity from this place.*

Go to the house spirit place and say,

> *House spirit, you are the soul of this place. Aid me in this rite as I banish all evil and negativity from this place.*

Go to your altar. Light the white candle and say,

> *Powers of fire, aid me in this rite as I banish all evil and negativity from this place.*

Light the incense and say,

> *Powers of air, aid me in this rite as I banish all evil and negativity from this place.*

Touch the bowl of water and say,

> *Powers of water, aid me in this rite as I banish all evil and negativity from this place.*

Add the salt to the bowl of water and say,

> *Powers of earth, aid me in this rite as I banish all evil and negativity from this place.*

Sprinkle yourself with the salt water and say,

> *May I be cleansed and purified, within and without.*

Put the incense (on a safe mat), bell, asperger, and the bowl of salt water on a tray. Take it with you and begin at the top of the house and work down to the back door. Repeat this procedure in each corner of each room:

Ring the bell and say,

> *In the name of the Lord and Lady, I command all evil and negativity to be gone. This do I will. So mote it be.*

Using the asperger, sprinkle the salt water into the corners of each room and say,

> *By the power of water I banish you. By the power of earth I banish you.*

Use the herb smoke to fumigate and say,

> *By the power of air I banish you. By the power of fire I banish you.*

Go to the centre of the room and ring the bell once, saying,

> *By the powers of earth, air, fire, and water, I command all evil and negativity to be gone.*

Ring the bell once more and say,

> *In the names of the hearth goddess and the house spirit, protectors and guardians of this place, I command all evil and negativity to be gone.*

Ring the bell for the third time and say,

> *In the names of the Lord and Lady, I banish all evil and negativity. So mote it be.*

When you have worked your way through each room (including pantries and broom closets), go to the top of the house and begin closing the doors and windows. As you do, using your forefinger, use the salt water to draw a protective pentagram at each entrance to the home (the external doors, windows, and air vents). Then, using a protection oil (page 80), dip in your finger and draw it around the edges of all the doors and windows, saying,

> *In the name of the Lord and Lady, I seal this place so that no evil may enter. This do I will. So mote it be.*

· · · · ·

Go to your hearth and say,

> *Hearth goddess, grant me your protection, as I give you my thanks and my service, so mote it be.*

Go to your house spirit place and say,

> *House spirit, grant me your protection, as I give you my thanks and my service, so mote it be.*

Visualise your home being filled with pure white light. Say,

> *Lord and Lady, god and goddess, bless my home and fill it with love. So mote it be.*

CHAPTER 5

· · · · · · · · · · · · · · · ·

Warding

In old cottages, you might find various things hanging up around the house—a horseshoe over the door, horse brasses on the hearth, or glass balls in the windows. These are not just decorations; they are wards for magical protection. Their purpose is to turn away negativity and evil.

We all want to protect our homes; we fit locks and security cameras to deter thieves and those who would intrude on the very place where we should feel safest, where we should be able to keep out what we don't want. Within living memory, it was also common to protect the home with magical wards—charms and spells to keep it safe and lucky. As witches, it is part of our craft to take basic precautions against harmful spiritual energies. Failing to do so would be like not bothering to lock the front door.

It is important to remember that we want to lock the magical door to keep out the undesirable while still letting in (and out) what is desirable. Warding spells must be carefully thought out and performed; you don't want the spirits you invoke unable to get in, and the spells you cast unable to get out. You will be faced with a magical void otherwise.

We only want to ward against what I am going to call negative energies, a catchall term that encompasses random unwanted spiritual or psychic intrusions, magic and malice sent against you, the disturbed energy of place, or atmospheres created by the spiritual residue of conflict.

First, we need to do a cleansing or banishing, because we don't want to lock bad stuff in with us. Once you have cleansed, it is time to prepare and place your wards. Wards will need to be placed at all the possible entry points—all the thresholds: the doorstep, doors, windows, air vents, chimney, and hearth.

When we make a ward, we use a physical object chosen for its intrinsic power, as well as what we will empower into it, to act as an anchor for the ward in the physical world and keep the magic working. This might be a bottle or jar we fill with specific objects, a horseshoe, a broomstick—all manner of things have been used traditionally.

Wards need regular maintenance, cleansing, and empowerment. Neglected, they may stop working. They may become exhausted and need replacing.

Empowering Wards

When you have chosen or made your ward object, it must be empowered, otherwise it is just an object. Begin by cleansing it with water or smoke fumigation. Then visualise as clearly as you can what you want the ward to do—protect you and deflect negativity. It is important that you make this as simple and clear as you can, as mixed or imprecise messages can be disastrous in magic. Then it is time to mentally gather that energy and project it into the object, thus combining the intrinsic power of the object and your own power. As you release the energy, it might help to say something like,

> *Guard and protect this house, so mote it be.*

or,

> *Deflect all negativity from this place and all who live here. So mote it be.*

Warding the Doorstep

The threshold of a house is a liminal place, neither inside nor outside, but a boundary between the two, and therefore vulnerable, a way for the otherworld to intrude. In British folklore, it was thought unlucky to tread on the threshold itself, and people were always careful to step over it; this is why brides, in a transitional stage of life, are carried across it. The Irish scattered primroses on the doorsteps to keep fairies from crossing it, and in England thresholds were made of protective holly wood for the same reason. The following methods may be used to protect the threshold.

Step Patterns

In parts of Britain, defensive designs called step patterns were drawn on the doorstep in salt or chalk or reproduced in mosaic or tiles. These took the form of knotwork and "tangled thread" patterns since spirits are said to follow straight paths when travelling and get caught up in trying to follow the twisting lines. You can protect your threshold by using white chalk or paint to inscribe protective runes, pentacles, knotwork, or tangled patterns on the doorstep.

Iron Filings

Iron filings may be laid in a line on the threshold. They draw on the power of iron to repel malicious magic and spirits.

Salt

Though it has the power to cleanse, purify, and protect, as well as being a symbol of hospitality, salt is also immensely damaging to plant and animal life when scattered on the earth. Do not lay salt on the grass or on the earth or you will kill what is there and offend the earth and its spirits. It should only be used for protection in extremis; it forms a barrier to all spiritual energies, good and bad, and is used to keep malicious energies out and never to encompass benevolent energies. You cannot invoke anything into salt! And it doesn't matter what kind of salt you use—table salt will work very well.

Witch Bottle

Historical witch bottles, dating back to the seventeenth century, have been found in cottages, colleges, inns, ecclesiastical premises, and historical buildings buried beneath the floor, under the threshold, near the hearth, or up a chimney—entry and exit points of the building and therefore more susceptible to ingress by dark supernatural forces, witches, ghosts, fairies, and demons. It was usual to get one of the cunning folk to create it.

Witch bottles were used for protection from magical attack or from disease. Each was found stoppered and filled with an assortment of items such as iron nails, lead shot, bundles of hair, thorns, and small bones. These are all protective items, and iron in particular is inimical to evil witches and fairies. The bottles were then filled with the final ingredient, the urine of the victim (the person who needed protection from magical attack) to bind the bottle to its creator, stoppered, and buried.

As well as protection from bewitchment, the witch bottle was used for protection against disease. A plastic witch bottle in the Museum of London found in the Thames seems to date from 1982, according to one coin found within it. It is filled with slivers of metal, coins, a tiny bottle of clove oil, and a large number of human adult teeth. It appears to have been aimed at protection from toothache or tooth decay, since clove oil is a remedy for toothache.[2]

Witches still make witch bottles. Some may baulk at using their own urine, but protective spikey items such as thorns and nails may be used in them, as well as strands of your hair or nail clippings. These personal objects bind the bottle to you.

To make your own witch bottle, take a glass bottle or jar with a lid and fill it with sharp nails, thorns, broken glass, and tangled threads plus some of your hair or nail clippings, saying,

> *Lord and Lady, in your name*
> *I fill this jar to protect my home*
> *With tangled thread to lay false trail*
> *And in defence a sharpened nail*
> *This glass deflects all bad intent*
> *On this shield all ill be spent.*

If you can, bury the bottle beneath your front step or the path that approaches it, or place it in the porch or beside the door with the words,

> *I bury [place] this charm*
> *To keep me from harm*
> *Hidden from sight to all but me.*
> *Lord and Lady, blessed be.*

The bottle will do its work protecting your home for as long as you leave it in place.

Warding the External Doors

Use these simple methods to boost your home's safety.

BROOM

Country and cunning folk would hang a broom above the front door to keep evil spirits out or cross brooms in front of the door to keep negative energy and malicious magical practitioners at bay. I keep a broom on my porch as a ward.

---

2 Learn more at https://www.museumoflondon.org.uk/discover/sorcery-display-witch-bottles.

PROTECTIVE DOOR WREATHS

In some parts of the world, it is traditional to hang decorative wreaths on the front door. Originally these were used for protective magic. You can combine several protective plants in one wreath to make a pleasing arrangement.

BIRCH TWIGS: protection, purification

BROOM: repels negativity

CEDAR: protection of place and people

CHILLIES: protective of people and possessions

CINNAMON STICKS: protection

CLOVE: stopping the evil eye

ELM TWIGS: protection from supernatural forces

EUCALYPTUS TWIGS AND LEAVES: protection, dispelling negativity

FIG: nurturing, protection

GARLIC: wards off negativity and the evil eye

GORSE: protection against evil witches

HAWTHORN: warding magic

HAZEL: peace, protection

HEATHER: repels negative influences

HOLLY: protection against bewitchment and evil spirits

IVY: safeguards property

LEMON: repels the evil eye

MISTLETOE: protection against lightning, disease, fires, and misfortunes

POMEGRANATE: drives out negative energies, wards off evil spirits

PRIMROSE: protects against evil spirits

ROSEMARY: protects the home

ROWAN: banishes undesirable entities

SAGE: protection

WILLOW TWIGS AND LEAVES: protection for the home

HAGSTONES

These are naturally holed stones, usually found on seashores or riverbanks, associated with the hag goddess herself and long believed to have a protective influence. A naturally holed stone is a ring, a circle of power. They may still sometimes be seen hanging in barns, stables, and other farm buildings throughout the UK. Sometimes a small one is added to the property's bunch of keys or hung over the keyholes.

HORSESHOES

Horseshoes draw on the power of iron to repel malicious magic and spirits. They are nailed above doors to protect the entrance to the home, hung with points upward as a sign of power.

NAILS

Hammered ceremonially into woodwork, especially doorframes, iron nails are a means of warding off bad luck and harm from households. Like horseshoes, they have the protective power of iron. Nails are symbols of binding harmful forces, literally "nailing the problem."

Warding the Windows

Windows and glass doorways are protected with wards such as the ones following and sealed with protection oil (page 80) smeared around the frame.

MIRRORED OBJECTS

Small mirrored ornaments may be hung in the window, facing outward to reflect any negativity back to where it came from.

EYES

Small glass or ceramic representations of eyes deflect the evil eye or malice sent against you.

WITCH BALL

Witch balls are hollow spheres of glass or polished metal that are hung in the window for protection, to deflect evil spirits, bad luck, negative energies, and magic sent against the homeowner. They had a widespread historical use in England (and later America) and are still found today in houses and shops. I've seen examples that are (roughly spherical) glass bottles, glass fishing floats, and very expensive purpose-made glass orbs. In the past, the balls were filled with coloured threads so that any spirit trying to enter would be forced to follow the thread and get lost, or sometimes they contained holy water or salt. A friend, who is a specialist charm maker, makes beautiful witch balls of reflective metal spheres hung below with various coloured ribbons, each of which has a specific purpose.

You can purchase purpose-made witch balls or glass fishing net floats, or just hang a few glass Christmas baubles in the window with these words:

> *Now I hang this shielding sphere*
> *To prevent all harm from entering here*
> *Lord and Lady with this charm*
> *I pray you keep my home from harm.*

COLOURED SPIRAL GLASS PAPERWEIGHT SPIRIT TRAP

When they have been magically empowered, glass objects containing spirals of colour serve to confuse spirits and dissipate harmful energies. Most common are ornamental paperweights.

Warding the Hearth

The hearth is a threshold too. The hearth is traditionally warded in the following ways.

WITCH MARKS

A common folk ward was the so-called witch mark. Rather than being a defence against witches, they were for general protection and found carved into the posts or stones near liminal places such as doors and hearths. They have been discovered dating back to the medieval period on barns, churches, and houses. One of the most common is the hexafoil, or "daisy wheel," boxes, meshes, and grids. These function as spirit traps.

HORSE BRASSES

You might still see horse brasses hung on the hearth in old pubs and houses. They were originally defensive charms attached to horse harnesses to protect the animals from enchantment, but since then they have been used as hearth wards. Traditional designs include lucky symbols such as the sun or moon, horseshoes, stars and wheels, or apotropaic (evil-repelling) symbols like serpents, lions, and dogs.

HAZEL CROSS

If you leave the fire unlit for any length of time, such as during the summer, place a protective equal-armed cross of hazel bound with red thread upon it.

WITCH POSTS

These were built into fireplaces in the north of England to prevent evil coming down the chimney to enter the hearth and home and to keep away evil witches. It was said that a witch could not pass the rowan wood post and the cross carved upon it, or the crooked silver sixpence that was kept in a hole at the centre of the post. The sixpence itself had magical properties, and if the butter would not turn, you prised it out and put it in the churn.

Additional Wards

Some extra wards for your magical arsenal:

ROWAN AND RED THREAD

A traditional charm to protect a home or barn involved a rowan cross tied with red thread. Rowan protects from evil magic and negative influences. To make one, take two pieces of rowan wood and a length of red thread. Tie the rowan sticks into an equal-armed cross (a solar symbol representing the solstices and equinoxes) with the red thread. Empower it by saying with each knot,

> *Hear me, sacred rowan wood*
> *Keep out evil, let in good*
> *By the knots in this red thread*
> *I call in peace and banish dread.*

Hang it in the highest place on your property.

Glass Walking Sticks (Charm Wands)

Glass has a magic all its own and is widely found in traditional wards. Glass walking sticks, which obviously cannot be used as a walking aid, were also called charm wands, medicine rods, witch canes, or witch's sticks. They seem to have been manufactured specifically for magical use. Most of them were made by the Nailsea glassworks in Somerset from 1788 to 1873. (Nailsea also manufactured witch balls.)[3]

They were hung on the wall, over entryways to prevent harm entering, or in a bedroom between the bed and the fireplace to absorb the spirits that caused disease, particularly the ague (rheumatism). They contained spiral patterns so that spirits would be trapped within them.[4] They had to be cleaned carefully each morning to remove any evil that had attached itself to them, and to break one would certainly cause bad luck. They were hung on the wall and dusted daily to keep away sprites and bad luck.[5] Each morning, the charm wand must be empowered by wiping it vigorously with a dry cloth whilst chanting a spell of empowerment. This charges up the wand, causing it to attract harmful particles to its surface, preventing the owner breathing them in and suffering illness as a result.

You'd be very lucky to find a Nailsea glass walking stick now, but I have found twisted glass rods in craft shops and even garden centres, complete with spiral patterns, that may be used as charm wand wards.

Glass Rolling Pin

Glass rolling pins may be used as wards. Historically, they were filled with salt, herbs, or tangled threads or beads and hung in the kitchen to deflect negativity.

Warding the Bedroom

The bedroom requires special consideration. Many people considered themselves most vulnerable in their bedrooms; after all, this is the place where we sleep and dream. The ancients had images of protective or benevolent gods in their bedrooms, such as a mask of the sun or the kindly Egyptian god Bes, who was thought to repel any evil spirits that attempted to enter the house.

---

3 Colquhoun, *The Living Stones*.
4 Colquhoun, *The Living Stones*.
5 Pennick, *The Ancestral Power of Amulets, Talismans and Mascots*.

If you are suffering from nightmares, consider doing a house cleansing to remove any negativity, and then set protective wards.

Horseshoe

It was common cottage practice to hang horseshoes at the foot of the bed to ward off nightmares.

Sprig of Thyme

Thyme wards off negativity and evil. Place a fresh sprig beneath your pillow to keep away nightmares.

Sprig of Rosemary

Rosemary is a powerfully protective herb. If you suffer from nightmares, place a sprig beneath your pillow.

Scrip against Nightmares

Assemble at the waxing moon.

> Blue pouch (blue represents tranquillity and peace)
>
> 1 dried bluebell flower (protects against nightmares and spirits)
>
> 1 teaspoon dried thyme (protects against nightmares)
>
> 1 teaspoon dried rosemary (protection from nightmares)
>
> 1 teaspoon dried peony petals (protection from nightmares)
>
> 1 teaspoon dried mullein leaves (protection from negative influences and evil spirits)
>
> Cedar (*Thuja*) essential oil (prevents nightmares)
>
> Red thread

As you place each ingredient into the bag, say,

> *Protect me and bless me.*

Tie up the scrip (pouch) with the thread. Hold it in your strongest hand and say,

> *Gods of protection* [you can name a deity you work with here, and if possible, have an image of this deity in your bedroom], *I have prepared this charm that I*

may be protected, and only good dreams may come to me. I charge this charm with love and blessing. So mote it be.

You can place the charm beneath your pillow or tie it to the bedpost.

Witch Bottle against Nightmares

Gather the following ingredients:

CERAMIC OR GLASS BOTTLE OR JAR WITH LID

5 HOLLY LEAVES (PROTECTION)

2 TEASPOONS FLAXSEEDS (WARDING OFF THE EVIL EYE)

1 TEASPOON THYME (PREVENTING NIGHTMARES)

BLUE AND RED THREAD

Take your glass bottle or jar and fill it with the ingredients, saying,

Mare, you shall not come
Till you have counted every flaxseed
Till you have counted all the fishes in the river
Till you have counted the leaves on every oak
Till you have travelled every tangled thread.

Place the bottle near the head of your bed with these words:

Lord and Lady
Wrap me in your cloak of protection
Keep me safe and grant me your blessings.
Blessed be.

Herbs for Home Warding

Some herbs have protective qualities that can be used in warding magic. (See appendix 8.) They can be used in a number of ways: hang bunches of the herbs in the house/outbuildings; use them in protective wreaths; have growing pots of herbs on your windowsills; add them to protective charms (scrips, bottles, etc.); use them in incense; or use them in magical oils to ritually seal doors and windows.

Part Two
Herb Cunning

Witchcraft and herbalism go hand in hand, and plant knowledge is the legacy of all the women who came before us. What a woman could grow or forage was a vital resource in times when there were few shops. From them she would make the family's preserves, wine and ale, and her cleaning and laundry products, inks, soaps, dyes, perfumes, and many other things. And let's not forget, when doctors were scarce or expensive, every woman kept her own stock of homemade herbal remedies to treat her family's ills and would make healing tea blends, poultices, distillations, tinctures, salves, and oils. Our ancestors would have found it very strange that we only use flowers for decoration. Women were highly skilled and amassed a vast amount of knowledge, though such knowledge was discounted and ignored by male scholars and doctors. It was women's magic, and all women had a bit of it.

Plants make up 99 percent of all life on earth; they are responsible for the air we breathe, the food we eat, and much of our modern medicine.[6] Despite this, most people ignore plants completely. Others just see them as commodities to be exploited.

But a plant is a living being, and each has its own personality. Because their lives are so different from ours—not moving, silent, rooted in one place—we might not even consider that they are alive, just as we are. Science is only just learning about the existence of plant sentience and plant communication, though this is something that witches, shamans, and many indigenous peoples have always recognised.[7]

---

6 Sibley, *Unveiling the Green.*
7 Learn more at https://academic.oup.com/book/51668/chapter-abstract/419696171?redirected
   From=fulltext.

For example, trees in a forest might seem to be individual, solitary plants, when in fact they are connected and communicate via a complex network of threadlike strands of fungi nicknamed the wood-wide web, and through this, the trees share food and water, sometimes sending supplies to sick trees, and warn each other about attacks from predators.[8] This reminds us how complex and interdependent ecosystems are.

Recognising that the vibrant web of life has many kinds of conscious beings changes how we think about the world. Animism, the belief that all beings have a relationship to one another and to Mother Earth, was once common to all societies. However, when later Western scholars came across it, they called it primitive and described animist cultures as primitive societies. We have increasingly become disconnected from nature, a dangerous illusion that damages our physical and spiritual well-being. Most people have no idea where their food comes from, or how it is produced, or what is in it. It is one of the reasons humankind has destroyed so many ecosystems, because we have not comprehended how interrelated they are and how much we depend on them.

The hearth witch seeks the wisdom of our green kin and strives to work together in harmony.

8 Learn more at https://www.bbc.co.uk/news/science-environment-48257315.

CHAPTER 6

· · · · · · · · · · · · · ·

Beginning to Work with Herbs

This section is intended to provide a basic introduction to the hearth witch's way of working with herbs. It is not within the scope of this volume to go into detail about individual herbs and preparations. I have written extensively about using herbs in cooking, self-care, medicine, and magic in the other books in this series.

What Is an Herb?

We use the word *herb* to refer to any plant we might use for medicine or magic, so this doesn't just include what we might traditionally think of as herbs, like basil and mint—plants that generally die down in winter—but also trees, shrubs, and flowers.

Obtaining Herbs

You can obtain herbs in many ways. You can forage for plants (wildcrafting), grow them in your garden, keep pots of herbs in your yard or on your kitchen windowsill, or buy dried herbs. You probably already have many herbs and spices in your kitchen cupboard that are useful for healing, personal care, and magic.

I recommend that you look at the environment around you and see what grows, because Mother Earth often ensures it is exactly what you need. Willow and meadowsweet are treatments for rheumatism and arthritis that grow in the damp environment where such conditions are more prevalent—Mother Earth knows what she is doing. Some of the most useful herbs are plants that people dismiss as weeds: dandelion, nettle, and so on. Use what you have, and don't chase expensive and exotic ingredients, which is not the wise woman way.

Harvesting Herbs

If you collect your own plant material, always use an open basket or cardboard box for harvesting to prevent crushing the material. Gather on a dry, sunny day. Always collect from healthy plants; don't pick damaged leaves or flowers. Leaves are best collected in spring or early summer, flowers as they bloom, berries as they become ripe, and roots in the autumn.

Double-check what you are harvesting to make sure you have identified the right plant. Don't mix different plants in your collecting basket.

Drying

You will need to attend to any plants you have collected quickly before they start to deteriorate. You can dry plants either by hanging them or spreading them flat on absorbent paper in a warm place or using a dehydrator or drying them in a very low oven. If you are harvesting the whole aerial parts of a plant (such as a bunch of nettles), you can make small bunches of stems and hang them up out of direct sunlight. When dry, crumble them into paper bags or dark glass jars as soon as possible.

Large flowers can be separated out on trays to dry. Leave enough air circulation between them. When dry, separate the petals.

Berries can be dried in a warmed oven, which is turned off before the trays of fruits are put in. Leave for three to four hours with the door of the oven open.

Roots should be gathered in autumn, washed, and chopped into small pieces. Spread on a tray and put in a warmed oven, turned off, for two to three hours.

Seeds can be collected by hanging the seeding heads of flowers upside down in a paper bag. They will fall to the bottom of the bag as the plant dries.

Storing

Badly stored plant material will soon deteriorate and lose its potency. Store in sterilised dark glass containers with airtight lids. If you don't have dark glass jars, you can wrap thick paper around the outside of clear jars. Do not use metal or plastic containers.

Getting Started

If you begin to read about herbs, you soon will realise just how much there is to know and become overwhelmed by the vastness of the subject. There are around fifty thousand plants that are used medicinally across the world, which means that you can't possibly have intimate knowledge of every useful herb. Even a really experienced medical herbalist might only use a few hundred.

A good way to begin is to take three or four herbs and try to learn as much as you can about them. It is best if they are herbs you have easy access to. Most wise women will concentrate on their local plants and the ones they grow themselves. Cook with your chosen herbs; make teas, salves, and poultices with them; experiment safely and document the results. When you are happy with your knowledge of those four herbs, add another two. Don't try to learn everything at once, and don't try to take it too quickly; maybe add another two or three each year, and then you won't forget what you have learned. Those plants will become permanent allies in your work.

Healing Plants

Wise women believe that Mother Nature, in her wisdom, gave us an herb for every ill. People have been investigating the properties of herbs for thousands of years in every country of the world, through trial, error, and observation, so we know a great deal, though there is always more to be discovered.

Herbs were once the only medicines we had, and even today, the World Health Organisation estimates that 80 percent of the world's population relies on plant medicine as their primary health care.[9] In the West, as we moved away from our close relationship with nature, that knowledge was sidelined and widely forgotten or dismissed as old wives' tales.

But old wives' tales usually have a basis in fact. It was a Shropshire wise woman who introduced English physician William Withering to the use of foxglove (*Digitalis* spp.) to successfully treat dropsy (swelling from congestive heart failure).[10] In 1785, he published a paper on foxglove's effects and toxicity. The prescription drug digoxin is still made from foxgloves and is still used for fluid buildup in congestive heart failure and irregular heartbeats. (Foxglove is deadly and should not be used by home herbalists.)

Many of our current pharmaceutical drugs are based on herbs. People have used willow bark and meadowsweet for thousands of years to treat pain and rheumatism. The English clergyman Edward Stone carried out the first scientific study of willow bark in 1763, when he successfully used it to treat ague in his parishioners. Scientists set out to analyse the active ingredient (salicylic acid) and create it synthetically. In 1859, German chemist Felix Hoffman produced pure stable acetylsalicylic acid, the first time a drug had been made synthetically. It was registered as Aspirin in 1899. The name is a combination of acetyl and spirea (*Spirea ulmaria* or meadowsweet).[11]

We use healing herbs all the time without realising it: we drink stimulating tea and coffee; we grate digestive black pepper onto our meals; we put antimicrobial, antiviral, and antifungal basil on our pasta; we put nausea-reducing ginger into our cakes; and so on. You might go further and drink a cup of peppermint tea to aid your digestion or take chamomile tea before bed to help you sleep.

---

9   Learn more at https://www.sciencedirect.com/science/article/abs/pii/B978012814619400001X#:~: text=According%20to%20World%20Health%20Organization,their%20primary%20health%20care%20 needs.

10 Learn more at https://www.britannica.com/biography/William-Withering.

11 Learn more at https://worldneurologyonline.com/article/controversial-story-aspirin/.

It is not within the scope of this book to go into detail on specific herbs and their preparation for healing, but I have written extensively on the subject in some of the other hearth witch books in this series.

Safety

Using herbs is not a replacement for modern medicine. You would be foolish to reject the benefits of properly used antibiotics, for example. Herbs can help, but there are limits to what they can do. However, there are herbs the hearth witch can use to treat everyday minor illnesses, and in some cases, these can be more effective than over-the-counter drugs. Ginger, for example, is more effective in treating nausea than most pharmaceuticals, while a honey and lemon drink, with a little glycerine, is better than any cough syrup you can purchase. Herbs can help support healing in more serious illnesses, but this should only be done in consultation with your healthcare professional and a qualified medical herbalist. Always consult a medical practitioner if you have any acute or persistent health concerns; never try to diagnose your own illness.

Don't assume that because herbs are natural they are safe and have no side effects. Even commonly used herbs can have ill effects in some individuals, depending on dosage, existing medical conditions, sensitivities, and allergies. Full-on allergic reactions are rare, but they can happen, because anyone can be allergic to anything. Do a twenty-four-hour skin test to check for sensitivities. Stop taking any herb immediately if you get a reaction such as dizziness, nausea, rashes, or headaches.

Some herbs should not be taken with other herbs or medications or by those suffering from particular medical conditions; it is important to check contraindications. Don't double dose; if you take sleeping tablets for example, don't take an herbal sleep aid too. Do not take any herb in medicinal amounts for an extended period. When you are pregnant, you should avoid medicinal quantities of herbs to be on the safe side.

Identify your herb properly. The name marigold is applied to *Calendula officinalis*, a useful medicinal herb, but also to *Tagetes*, an annual flower used as a bedding plant which is poisonous. Get a good herbal and a good plant identification guide. If possible, take a course on plant identification, particularly if you plan on foraging your herbs. Pick your herbs from unpolluted locations.

Beware of buying herbs and supplements from unknown suppliers on the internet; what you get might not be what you think you are buying. When buying from a shop, be aware that they may have had their stock on the shelves for a long time, and the herbs might have lost their potency.

Make sure that you have looked up the method of preparation and the safe dosages.

Standardised Extracts

I avoid taking herbs in commercially available capsules. These products contain standardised extracts of the active ingredients, making them akin to pharmaceutical drugs. Traditional herbalists seek to use the whole plant, which is better utilised by the body and comes with its own buffers, checks, and balances. Dandelion, for example, is a useful diuretic. While pharmaceutical diuretics rob the body of potassium and require supplementation with potassium when used, whole dandelion is a source of potassium and provides more potassium than is lost by urination.

Herb Simples

An herb simple is a medicine made from a single herb and water, and it is one of the easiest ways to start working with healing herbs. An herb simple can be an herb tea, an infusion (a greater proportion of herb to boiling water than a tea), or a decoction (the herb is boiled in water). If you can boil water, you can make an herbal remedy.

By using one herb rather than a combination of several, it is much easier to discern the effect of that plant, and if someone has a bad reaction to the remedy, it is obvious what the source of the distress is and usually easy to correct. The more herbs there are in a formula, the more likelihood there is of unwanted side effects. Combining herbs with the same properties is counterproductive and more likely to cause trouble than a simple.

Thirty Herb Teas for Healing

The following herbs are staples in the hearth witch's pantry:

CALENDULA (*CALENDULA OFFICINALIS*): activates the liver and aids in the digestion of fats.

CHAMOMILE (*MATRICARIA RECUTITA*): has a relaxing and sedative effect; used as a sleep aid and for stress and anxiety, digestive problems, and indigestion. May help premenstrual syndrome.

CRANBERRY (*VACCINIUM MACROCARPON*): drink for urinary tract infections.

DANDELION LEAF (*TARAXACUM OFFICINALE*): aids digestion and promotes appetite. It is diuretic and can be used to treat swollen ankles and fluid retention. For rheumatism and arthritis, take dandelion leaf tea to help the joints and aid the removal of acid deposits.

DANDELION ROOT (*TARAXACUM OFFICINALE*): a safe liver herb that stimulates bile production and is used in the treatment of jaundice, hepatitis, and urinary tract infections.

ECHINACEA (*ECHINACEA* SPP.): boosts the immune system and may reduce the duration of a cold.

ELDERBERRY (*SAMBUCUS NIGRA*): boosts the immune system and is useful for coughs, colds, and flu.

ELDERFLOWER (*SAMBUCUS NIGRA*): effective in bringing down the temperature and therefore is useful for flu and other infections where high temperature is a problem, such as measles. It also has antiviral properties and may benefit cases of bronchitis, sinusitis, and other catarrhal inflammations of the upper respiratory tract.

FENNEL (*FOENICULUM VULGARE*): gas pains, indigestion, and irritable bowel syndrome. Drink fennel seed tea twenty or thirty minutes before a meal to ease heartburn.

GINGER (*ZINGIBER OFFICINALE*): helpful for nausea and diarrhoea, motion sickness, indigestion, wind, and irritable bowel; loosens phlegm and helps clear mucus from the throat for colds and flu. For a sore throat, gargle with ginger tea.

JASMINE (*JASMINUM* SPP.): aids digestion and relieves flatulence, abdominal pain, diarrhoea, dyspepsia, and irritable bowel syndrome. Jasmine tea has a sedative effect on the nervous system and promotes peaceful sleep.

LAVENDER (*LAVENDULA* SPP.): has soothing effects on the central nervous system. Take for mild pain relief, to soothe nervous tension, or to act as a mild sedative before bed.

LEMON (*CITRUS LIMON*): supports the immune system, with antiseptic, astringent, and fever-reducing properties. Lemon is a staple in the treatment of coughs and colds. Lemon may help reduce inflammation in arthritic and rheumatic conditions. Lemon aids digestion and encourages the production of bile.

LEMON BALM (*MELISSA OFFICINALIS*): calming to the central nervous system. Used for anxiety, depression, tension, nervous palpitations, and anxiety-caused digestive problems, nervous headaches, anxiety, and mild depression.

LEMONGRASS (*CYMBOPOGON* SPP.): treats stress, anxiety, and insomnia. It also aids digestion, reduces bloating, and may help relieve a headache.

LINDEN FLOWER (*TILIA* SPP.): nerve tonic, calming and sedative. Useful in cases of anxiety and insomnia. It is diaphoretic (promotes sweating) and may help colds, flu, and fevers.

LIQUORICE ROOT (*GLYCYRRHIZA GLABRA*): sore throat, indigestion, heartburn, acid reflux, and peptic ulcers. Its expectorant (loosens phlegm) actions treat a cough and upper respiratory tract infections.

MARSHMALLOW LEAF (*ALTHAEA OFFICINALE*): treats indigestion, irritable bowel syndrome, a dry sore throat, a dry cough, and mild constipation.

NETTLE, STINGING (*URTICA DIOICA*): detoxes the blood, which can help with gout and arthritis.

PASSIONFLOWER (*PASSIFLORA* SPP.): treats anxiety, tension, nervousness, insomnia, and sleep issues. Passionflower acts as a mild sedative. The tea may be used for tension and pain. It can be particularly useful for menstrual cramping and premenstrual syndrome.

PEPPERMINT (*MENTHA PIPERITA*): treats indigestion, bloating, wind, nausea, headaches, and migraines.

PINE NEEDLE (*PINUS SYLVESTRIS*): has a mildly antiseptic effect within the chest. Useful for coughs.

ROSE (*ROSA* SPP.): mildly sedative, antidepressant, and anti-inflammatory. It may help period pain and menopausal symptoms.

ROSE HIP (*ROSA* SPP.): reduces the inflammation and pain associated with arthritis.

ROSEMARY (*ROSMARINUS OFFICINALIS*): eases dyspepsia caused by nervous tension and tension headaches caused by tight shoulders. Its anti-inflammatory and mild analgesic actions may be helpful for arthritis, rheumatic pain, and aching muscles. Rosemary improves memory.

SAGE (*SALVIA OFFICINALIS*): useful for coughs and colds, a gargle for sore throats, and tonsillitis. It helps those going through the menopause with hot flushes, night sweats, and other menopausal symptoms.

ST. JOHN'S WORT (*HYPERICUM PERFORATUM*): useful for headaches, nervous conditions, irregular menstruation, mild depression, and insomnia.

THYME (*THYMUS* SPP.): useful for coughs, colds, flu and bronchitis, indigestion, flatulence, irritable bowel syndrome, tension headaches, and hangovers.

VALERIAN ROOT (*VALERIANA OFFICINALIS*): calms stress, anxiety, hysteria, nervous tension, headaches, and migraines. Valerian root tea relieves insomnia and improves the quality of sleep.

YARROW (*ACHILLEA MILLEFOLIUM*): brings down the temperature and encourages sweating, so is useful for colds, flu, catarrh, rheumatism, and fever. Yarrow soothes digestion and stops diarrhoea. Yarrow contains the natural painkiller salicylic acid, so the tea is useful for headaches, menstrual cramps, and arthritis.

· · · · · · · · · · · · · ·

HERB TEA BASIC RECIPE

2 TEASPOONS FRESH HERBS OR 1 TEASPOON DRIED HERB

250 MILLILITRES WATER

Put the herbs in a teapot or a pot with a lid, pour in the boiling water and infuse for ten to twenty minutes. Strain and drink, sweetened with honey if desired. Take one to three times daily.

CHAPTER 7

· · · · · · · · · · · · ·

The Hearth Witch's Garden

Traditionally the wise woman's garden contained plants for food, herbs for the kitchen and for healing, dye plants, plants to delight the senses with beautiful colours and perfumes, plants to attract insects and feed familiars, plants to contact the spirits, plants for magic, divination, and spells, and trees like rowan and holly for protection. Week by week, month by month, season by season, the garden will have different rewards for me. I watch and wait and try to understand what Mother Earth is teaching me. Every year is different, and perhaps some of my old plant friends will have disappeared this year, and when that happens, I usually realise I no longer needed them, or perhaps new plant allies will have found their way to me. When a patch of weeds suddenly starts to grow where none were before, I stop to consider whether Mother Earth may be sending me exactly what I need at that moment, and she usually is.

I believe every single plant has its own unique gift of healing, food, or beauty, even—perhaps especially—the weeds. But all the plants here in my garden have their uses. I can eat carnation and peony petals, honeysuckle flowers, lilac blossoms, and fuchsia berries, and nasturtium seeds make a good substitute for capers. I can use the lawn daises to make a salve for bruises, while the dandelion is a detoxifying herb packed full of vitamins and minerals.

My scented geraniums are soothing for sore muscles and the heather flowers make a lovely tea that helps me sleep. Even after all these years I am still finding new ways to use all the garden gives me, so I honour each gift and embrace it fully by making herb simples, teas, salves, wines, cosmetics, oils, incenses, syrups, and vinegars.

The Garden as Sacred Space

We witches garden in a different way, because for us the garden is sacred space. We know that the garden is full of the power of the invisible. There are many spirits in the garden, gods and devas, and the intersecting spirits of animals and plants. The garden has its own soul, which I believe evolves from the matrix of all that has lived there—the people, animals, plants, and spirits—and the events that have happened there. When the spirit of the garden is acknowledged, its power awakens. I ask for its help to make the most of my garden as a place all its beings can share. When I am planning changes in the garden, when I am planting, weeding, and pruning, I ask it to oversee my work. I've said this before, but I always call gardening spiritual practice at its most raw, an instant connection to the mysteries of life. There is magic in the garden.

The Web of Life

I know that my garden doesn't belong to me: it belongs to nature. It's an interconnected web of life, from the microbes in the soil to the insects that pollinate the flowers, the birds that feed on the insects, and the small mammals that forage in the undergrowth. It teaches me about the interconnectedness and unity of all things. The garden is a gift of Mother Earth and Father Sun, cooled by Brother Wind, and nourished by Sister Rain. I share it with Brother Bee, Sister Butterfly, Brother Robin, and many more nonhuman kin. All their little lives go on there, and for some, it is the only home they know. I understand that the birds and mammals, the insects and even the slugs and snails have just as much right to this land as I do. We are all part of the same web and must learn to live in harmony with each other; you can't take one thing out of an ecosystem without adversely affecting every other part of it.

DEDICATION OF AN HERB GARDEN RITUAL

Have ready some mead and honey cakes (or vegan wine and cake if you wish) and four cornucopias (baskets or vases of flowers and fruit).

Start in the centre. Say,

> *Mother goddess, Earth Mother*
> *I honour this land and dedicate its purpose.*
> *Mother goddess, Melissa*
> *You are the queen bee*
> *The lady of honey, the sweetness of life*
> *You call the bees to the flowers*
> *To pollinate them, and make them fertile*
> *So that we shall have fruit and seeds*
> *Without you the earth is barren*
> *You are the sweetness of life*
> *You are life itself.*

Offer the mead by pouring it on the earth and place the cakes on the ground. Say,

> *I make you this offering, Melissa, lady of the bees*
> *To dedicate this land and its purpose*
> *In thanks for your messengers, the insects*
> *In thanks for their work*
> *We will honour them.*
> *Let blessing be.*

Go to the east corner and lay down the first cornucopia, saying,

> *Goddess, Earth Mother, lady of the herbs*
> *I come to honour you.*
> *I walk sunways around this place*
> *To consecrate and bless it.*
> *Earth Mother, you give of yourself.*
> *You sprout the seed and nurture the shoots.*
> *You open the flowers and set the fruit.*
> *I have prepared this offering in your honour*
> *Made from the wind and the rain*

The soil and the sun made manifest
Grown from your womb.
I bless and consecrate this place in your name and in your honour.

Repeat in the south, the west, and finally the north. Then say,

Let this ritual end with love and blessings. Blessed be.

CHAPTER 8

. . . .

Herbs in Magic

While many people use herbs for cooking and some use them for healing, witches also employ herbs for magic.

The first thing to say is that we don't *use* herbs in magic; we recognise the spirit in our green kin and ask that spirit to work with us, to become a partner in our magical work. The magic begins when we walk the land, when we choose the herb, when we make a connection with its spirit and the land allies around it.

Sometimes a plant or tree will call to you, and you should listen and trust your inner wisdom. Accept any insight that is given to you, no matter what the circumstances. No two ash trees have the same personality, and no two dandelions have exactly the same qualities. Some plants will share willingly, some must be courted, some will never give you anything, no matter how persistent you are. When we incorporate herbs in magic, it's not a case of following a kind of cookbook recipe, a pinch of this and a pinch of that. We need to harness the living power of plants, and that can only be done with the cooperation of the plant spirit.

The most important way you can work with an herb is season by season, observing it, listening for its spirit, trying to understand its gifts, and harmonising its spirit with your own when you both agree it is right to attain your goal. The plant itself is always the teacher.

Witches, indigenous shamans, and traditional healers have always understood the need to communicate with the plants they use.

Gathering Herbs for Magic

If the individual green kin is approached with love and trust, its energy may harmonise with you and share its secrets. If the plant is taken with the wrong motives or it is mistreated or misused, it may cause discomfort, mislead, or seek to gain control of the witch. If an enemy is made of the plant spirit, it can be destructive. When plant spirits share their gifts, we thank them from our hearts, and we might leave an offering if that feels suitable, but the offering should be something suitable that costs us thought and effort, and not just a matter of leaving useless litter. I find a sprinkle of compost is very acceptable to most plants!

Gather produce on a dry day, as any damp can have a tendency to turn to mildew. Do not use iron or steel to cut them, as it earths their life force, and don't let them touch the ground after they've been picked as this has the same effect.

Connecting with the Plant Spirits

To connect with our green kin, you must learn by practice and by using your inner senses.

Last summer I took a group out into my lavender patch and asked them what the first thing they noticed was. Some said the colour of the flowers, others said the scent, and a couple of people commented on the number of bees that seemed to be attracted to the flowers. I then asked the group to try to sense the energy of the plant. Almost everyone commented that it seemed very gentle. Indeed, the energy of lavender is always gentle. A lavender tea or salve will sooth and heal small cuts or burns and soothe skin irritations. If you drink lavender tea, it will soothe nervous tension and can help you sleep. Several people commented that it felt very powerful, but its power was calm, peaceful, generous, and giving. Lavender can calm our anxiety and lift us from the doldrums when we are sad. Finally, I asked them to ask the lavender if she was willing to share her gifts. Everyone said yes. Most plants, if approached in the right way, are willing to become your ally, take you by the hand, and show you what, together, you are capable of.

To connect with your green kin, spend time with the plants, noting where they live—in sun or shade, on chalky soil or sandy soil and so on—their growth habits, when they flower, and when they set their seeds. Note the shape of the leaves, their texture and colour, their taste, if edible. In this way you will begin to learn from the plants themselves. You must learn to speak the language of each plant spirit by listening with an open heart and using your inner senses, as well as the everyday senses of taste, smell, and touch (if it is safe to do so). Don't expect to learn everything at once, as it will likely be over several seasons that the plant reveals its nature to you.

Herbal Correspondences

To know what herb to use for a particular magical act, we can use our senses; the herbs that come in spring can be used for spring festivals, and their youthful energy speaks of vibrancy and new beginnings. Rayed golden flowers vibrate with the energy of the sun, strength, power, and healing. Night-blooming flowers resonate with the mysterious energy of the moon, and so on. Earth plants tend to be nourishing, like oats and wheat, or earthy smelling, like patchouli or vetiver, so we use them for magic of manifestation and health. Plants of air tend to be freshly fragrant, such as mint, rosemary, and lavender, or light and airy, like poplar and aspen, and we use them for magic of thought and communication. Water plants are juicy and fleshy or grow near water, and their energy is associated with what flows—the emotions, feelings, and subconscious, and water magic is often concerned with divination and scrying. Fire plants tend to have fiery sap or taste hot like ginger or have warm perfumes, like carnation, clove, and cinnamon. Fire gives us vitality, igniting action, animation, and movement. It sparks courage and acts of bravery. It heats passion and enthusiasm. Fire magic is concerned with creativity, life energy, and zeal.

If you look up the herbal correspondences of a plant, you may read that such and such an herb is ruled by the sun or Mercury and so on. For at least a couple of thousand years and right up to the seventeenth century and beyond, it was usual for physicians to take astrological influences into account when formulating treatments for their patients based on which planet had caused the disease or which part of the body was afflicted. They believed that all herbs and plants came under the rulership of the planets. Herbs ruled by the sun, for example, turn toward the sun or have yellow flowers, like marigold, St. John's wort, and dandelion; they were used to promote vitality.

Mars is the planet of war, so Mars plants symbolise a warlike spirit and generally have thorns or stings, like thistles and nettles, and they were used to treat muscular complaints. Saturn is the planet of aging, limitation, and death, so Saturn plants are slow growing or long living and woody, thrive in the shade, have deep roots, or are poisonous, foul smelling, or considered evil, such as hemlock and henbane. Some of them were used to treat teeth and bones.

In astrology, Mercury is the planet of communication, so Mercury plants include fast-growing weeds, creepers, and winding plants, or plants with hairy, fuzzy, or finely divided leaves. They may be aromatic. They were used to treat the brain and the five senses. Venus is, of course, the planet of love and beauty, so Venus plants overwhelm the senses with sweet scents and lovely flowers, red fruits, or soft, furry leaves. They were used to treat the reproductive organs.

When we think of the moon, it governs the tides, so moon plants often grow near water or have a high water content or juicy leaves. They were used to treat the digestive system. They may have white flowers or moon-shaped leaves or seedpods. Jupiter is the bringer of abundance, and Jupiter plants are usually big and bold and often edible. They were used to promote growth and nourish the liver.

This was something male physicians incorporated into their science, which was forbidden to women. The wise women worked very differently, using the knowledge passed down from their ancestors and teachers, their own observations, and the close relationships they formed with plant spirits to decide what herbs to use, whether for healing or for magic.

Incorporating Herbs in Magic

Books can give you a good starting place, but we only really learn our craft by doing. There are hundreds of ways you can bring your hearth witch's herb craft into your magical work: making ritual wine and food, potions and brews, or talismans, scrips, witch bottles, wards, amulets, charms, spells, teas, potions, incense, and oils.

RITUAL FUMIGATION

One of the simplest ways of cleansing your home of negative energy is to use a smoking bundle of herbs or carry a dish of herbs burning on charcoal as you walk from room to room. The practice of burning herbs to cleanse and purify a place is common throughout the world. Various herbs have been used, such as sage, juniper, and frankincense. Remember that white sage is spiritually significant to certain Native American tribes and endangered, so consider alternatives. (See appendix 9.)

Incense

We use incense for many magical purposes. It is a traditional offering to please the Gods. In ritual or for meditation, we can use it to set the mood required for ritual or magic and concentrate the mind on the task at hand. The fragrance of the incense might be stimulating or calming, soothing or invigorating, according to what herbs we incorporate. Moreover, we use the combined vibrational force of the chosen plants for specific magical operations.

Many people use joss sticks and incense cones, but these are often made from synthetic ingredients and have no intrinsic magical value. I much prefer to make my own loose incense. I know it incorporates the correct ingredients blended in the proper manner at the right magically empowering time.

Making Incense

You can make incense from any kind of plant material: resins, barks, seeds, dried flowers, dried leaves, and dried roots. (Just make sure they don't release a toxic vapour.) You can also add 100 percent pure essential oils. It is, however, much more powerful if you make them using ingredients you have collected mindfully, prepared, and empowered yourself.

To make an incense, assemble your ingredients, your pestle and mortar, your mixing spoons, and your jars and labels. Lay out the tools and ingredients on the altar, lighting a candle. If you are using resins and essential oils, these should be combined first, stirring lightly with the pestle and left to go a little sticky before you add any woods, barks, and crushed berries. Next add any herbs and powders and lastly any flowers. As you blend the incense, concentrate on the purpose for which the incense will be used, consecrating with these words:

> *Father Sun and Mother Earth, bless this incense, which I would consecrate in your*
> *names. Let it obtain the necessary virtues for acts of love and beauty in your honour.*
> *Let blessing be.*

Burning Loose Incense

To use your incenses, take a self-igniting charcoal block (available from occult and church suppliers) and apply a match to it. It will begin to spark across its surface, and eventually to glow red. Place it on a flameproof dish with a mat underneath (it will get very hot). When the charcoal block is glowing, sprinkle a pinch of the incense on top; a little goes a long way. Alternatively, if you are celebrating outdoors and have a bonfire, you can throw much larger quantities of incense directly into the flames.

Incense Recipes

All the measurements for incense in this book are by volume, not weight. Use a spoon to measure out small quantities when making a single jar of incense. Therefore, if the recipe says three parts frankincense, half part basil, and one part rosemary, this means three spoons of frankincense, half a spoon of basil, and one spoon of rosemary.

HOUSE SPIRIT INCENSE

Blend at a waxing or full moon.

3 PARTS FRANKINCENSE RESIN

1 PART ROSEMARY

½ PART BASIL

½ PART SALT

¼ PART WHEAT

HOUSE BLESSINGS INCENSE

Blend during a waxing moon.

3 PARTS FRANKINCENSE RESIN

½ PART GRAIN (WHEAT, RYE, BARLEY, ETC.)

½ PART HONEY (OPTIONAL)

¼ PART SALT

1 PART LAVENDER FLOWERS

½ PART LEMON BALM LEAVES

FEW DROPS LAVENDER OIL

FEW DROPS LEMON BALM OIL

House Cleansing Incense

Blend at a waning moon.

2 PARTS FRANKINCENSE RESIN

½ PART GARDEN SAGE

1 PART CRUSHED JUNIPER BERRIES

½ PART ROSEMARY

FEW DROPS ROSEMARY OIL

FEW DROPS EUCALYPTUS OIL

Banishing Incense

Blend at a waning moon.

½ PART ROWANBERRIES

3 PARTS FRANKINCENSE RESIN

½ PART RUE

½ PART JUNIPER NEEDLES

½ PART ST. JOHN'S WORT LEAVES AND FLOWERS

½ PART GARLIC POWDER

¼ PART CHILLI POWDER

Waxing Moon Incense

Blend during the waxing moon and use for workings connected with new beginnings—things that will grow to fullness in the future.

3 PARTS WHITE ROSE PETALS

1 PART FRANKINCENSE RESIN

½ PART WHITE LILY FLOWERS

¼ PART MUGWORT

. . . .

Full Moon Incense

Blend during the full moon for workings connected with positive magic—healing, blessing, and so on.

1 PART BENZOIN RESIN

2 PARTS MYRRH RESIN

2 PARTS FRANKINCENSE RESIN

3 PARTS WHITE SANDALWOOD

½ PART ORRIS ROOT POWDER

½ PART THYME

½ PART POPPY SEEDS

1 PART WHITE ROSE PETALS

½ PART GARDENIA FLOWERS

. . . .

Waning Moon Incense

Blend during the waning moon and use for workings connected with letting go, winding down, relinquishing old relationships and situations, purification, and cleansing magic.

½ PART ASPEN WOOD

½ PART BLACKBERRY LEAVES

½ PART WHITE CLOVER FLOWERS

½ PART ELDERFLOWERS

4 PARTS MYRRH RESIN

¼ PART PARSLEY

¼ PART WILLOW WOOD

Dark Moon Incense

Blend during the three days of the dark moon and use for workings of deep inner journeys and meditations.

½ PART PARSLEY

2 PARTS WILLOW BARK

3 PARTS MYRRH RESIN

½ PART FORGET-ME-NOT FLOWERS

Hearth Goddess Incense

3 PARTS FRANKINCENSE RESIN

½ PART DRIED ROWANBERRIES

1 PART BIRCH BARK

1 PART WILLOW WOOD

1 PART OAK WOOD

½ PART ROSE PETALS

½ PART LAVENDER FLOWERS

Crone Incense

5 PARTS MYRRH RESIN

2 PARTS ASPEN WOOD OR BARK

½ PART BLACKBERRY LEAVES OR WOOD

½ PART CRUSHED ELDERBERRIES

½ PART PARSLEY

1 PART WILLOW BARK

. . . .

Earth Mother Incense

3 PARTS PINE RESIN

2 PARTS BIRCHWOOD

1 PART PINEWOOD

½ PART ROSE PETALS

¼ PART VERVAIN

¼ PART HONEYSUCKLE FLOWERS

¼ PART MUGWORT LEAVES

FEW DROPS CYPRESS ESSENTIAL OIL

FEW DROPS OAKMOSS ESSENTIAL OIL

FEW DROPS PATCHOULI OIL

. . . .

Father Sun Incense

2 PARTS ACACIA RESIN

3 PARTS FRANKINCENSE RESIN

1 PART BENZOIN RESIN

½ PART ORANGE PEEL

2 PARTS SANDALWOOD

½ PART ROSEMARY

¼ PART CINNAMON BARK

FEW DROPS CEDAR ESSENTIAL OIL

FEW DROPS ORANGE ESSENTIAL OIL

. . . .

Consecration Incense

1 PART BENZOIN RESIN

½ PART MACE

½ PART STORAX

½ PART CLOVE

FEW DROPS FRANKINCENSE OIL

. . . . .

. . . .

LOVE INCENSE

3 PARTS FRANKINCENSE RESIN

1 PART MYRRH RESIN

¼ PART CRUSHED CARDAMOM PODS

¼ PART CINNAMON POWDER

½ PART ROSE PETALS

FEW DROPS JASMINE ESSENTIAL OIL

FEW DROPS ORANGE ESSENTIAL OIL

Magical Oils

When we use an oil for magic, we are using the inherent powers of that plant, so you cannot use synthetic oils for magic. You probably won't know what's in the synthetic oil, but it is not magically inert—what's in it will have its own energy and vibration, and that may have the opposite effect to the working you intend. You should never introduce an unknown quantity into a magical operation.

When you create a magical oil, you make it for a specific purpose, blending it with intent and choosing the ingredients very carefully to achieve a magical task. Do not take internally!

Magical oils can be made by blending essential oils or by creating your own macerated oils from fresh or dried plant material.

Magical oils are already imbued with the power of the plants and the intent you put into their blending, but before you use them, you can charge (or magically empower) them, which reinforces their purpose. Taking your wand or just your forefinger, tap the bottle and say,

> Let the Lord and Lady witness
> That I charge this oil
> That it may [state purpose]

. . . .

PROTECTION OIL

20 MILLILITRES OLIVE OIL

3 DROPS ROSEMARY ESSENTIAL OIL

4 DROPS ROSE GERANIUM ESSENTIAL OIL

4 DROPS CYPRESS ESSENTIAL OIL

. . . .

SELF-BLESSING OIL

30 MILLILITRES SUNFLOWER OIL

2 DROPS BERGAMOT ESSENTIAL OIL

2 DROPS CLOVE ESSENTIAL OIL

6 DROPS ROSE ESSENTIAL OIL

2 DROPS CARDAMOM ESSENTIAL OIL

5 DROPS ORANGE ESSENTIAL OIL

. . . .

FULL MOON OIL

Blend at the full moon and use as an anointing oil for full moon rituals, to anoint tools and spells.

20 MILLILITRES ALMOND OR OLIVE OIL

10 DROPS SANDALWOOD ESSENTIAL OIL

4 DROPS FRANKINCENSE ESSENTIAL OIL

10 DROPS ROSE ESSENTIAL OIL

. . . .

RELINQUISHING OIL

Blend under the full moon.

20 MILLILITRES ALMOND OR OLIVE OIL

6 DROPS CYPRESS ESSENTIAL OIL

. . . .
Consecration Oil

30 MILLILITRES OLIVE OR SUNFLOWER OIL

4 DROPS BAY ESSENTIAL OIL

4 DROPS BAYBERRY ESSENTIAL OIL

10 DROPS FRANKINCENSE ESSENTIAL OIL

. . . .
Rose Macerated Oil

Simply pack a clean glass jar with strongly scented, lightly crushed, rose petals. Cover with a light oil, such as grapeseed or sunflower, and put in a dark place for a week, shaking daily. Strain the oil from the petals onto fresh petals and repeat. Keep repeating this process until the oil takes on the strength of scent you desire. Use in love magic, spells, rituals, incense, oils, talismans, and charms.

. . . .
Violet Oil

Pack violet leaves and flowers into a clean glass jar. Cover them with oil. Put on the lid and place on a sunny windowsill for two weeks, shaking daily. Strain the macerated oil into a sterilised jar, fit the lid, and label. Will keep eight to twelve months. Use to honour goddesses of love, and for love spells, and to anoint love-attracting amulets.

Magical Bath Salts

Take a cup of cooking salt, add sixteen to twenty drops of the required oils, and blend with the back of a spoon. Store immediately in an airtight container and add a handful to your ritual bath for cleansing the body and aura and to help you attune to the matter at hand.

. . . .
Waning Moon Purification Bath

Blend at the waning moon.

2 HANDFULS SALT

FEW DROPS ROSEMARY OIL

FEW DROPS FRANKINCENSE OIL

Holding your hand over the blend, bless it with these words:

> *Goddess of the waning moon*
> *Who cleanses and purifies*
> *Bless this salt*
> *Created in your honour.*

Store the salt in an airtight container. Use a handful in your bath during the waning moon to cleanse the body and aura. Before you get into the bath, say,

> *May I be cleansed within and without*
> *And release all that no longer serves me*
> *Let all hindrance*
> *Be washed away.*
> *By the waning moon goddess*
> *So mote it be.*

Relax in the bath for a while. When you pull the plug, imagine all you wish to be rid of flowing down the drain.

Part Three
Working with the Gods

In our materialistic society, the earth, rocks, rivers, plants, and animals have become just things to us—things we can use, or things that are useless to us and may be ignored. For all our ancestors, every river was a god, every tree held a spirit, and every animal was its own unique being. The whole world—and everything in it—was alive; it shone with meaning, magic hummed in the air, and the Gods were imminent in the land. In our disenchanted world, awe and wonder have been stripped away, and so many people feel a sense of alienation, of spiritual and emotional loss, because they are cut off from our divine source. When we approach the world, mindful of its inherent sacredness, it becomes a magical place, vibrantly animate and full of wonder, where Mother Earth creates and re-creates. In it, we connect to something greater than ourselves, because the spiritual and the physical are reflections of each other.

Spiritual practice reminds us that we live in a sacred world and that we should strive to build a sacred relationship with it. We spend our ordinary lives trying to make connections—with lovers, friends, colleagues, and groups. Spiritual practice is about making connection with something that is greater than us, the powers underlying creation, whether we call these god, goddess, the Gods, cosmic consciousness, or simply spirit.

There is a divine energy that flows through all things and connects them as one. This energy is always flowing and always available to each one of us. This is the source of all our power, and when we connect with it and allow the divine to flow through us, we begin to work in harmony with the Gods and with all of creation.

So how do you begin to make spiritual connections?

First, you must be prepared to set aside your individual ego and recognise that you are one among many. There is a whole cosmos of beings, each with their own stories, paths, and concerns: plants, animals, rivers, mountains, deserts, seas, spirits, and gods. We are all related, and we can all connect with each other, learn from each other, and work in harmony with each other. This is ancient wisdom we have forgotten, but which we can rediscover. When you do, you will never look at the world in the same way again: it becomes enchanted and full of magic.

Then, as always with magic, be clear on what you are trying to achieve: your intent, forging connections with the spirit in all things and with the powers behind creation, the Gods. Then you begin to act on that intent with offerings, ceremony, ritual, chanting, prayer, and meditation. These practices form an energetic link between the material (you, your home, and your magical working space) and the Gods. At first, you may struggle or fail to make connections, but with persistence and repetition, the links will gradually be formed. There is no shortcut to building a relationship with the Gods. No one can open the way for you, and you must do it for yourself.

The outward forms of practice are adaptable and can be very simple or complex, from the simple lighting of a candle with intent to a full-on formal ritual. In this book I offer you a few suggestions, but you may find your own ways that work better for you. When you bring your true self to your practice, the Gods respond.

It is tempting to try to force things and hurry them along, but the power will unfold at its own pace, and when you are ready for it.

CHAPTER 9

. . . .

Personal Practice

You will never contact the Gods while your mind is cluttered with mundane chatter. You must turn your attention away from the everyday world, thoughts, and emotions, and find the still, silent place within. Then, when you approach with reverence, the sacred can begin to communicate with you. Don't rush, stop trying to accomplish it, and learn to simply *be*.

Listening and Sensing Exercise

We are conditioned to be always busy, always doing, always communicating and talking, filling the time and space. We are afraid of stillness and silence. We feel guilty about it because in our culture, it seems alien. But stillness and silence are powerful ways of being.

Only when we stop talking and sit in stillness can we hear voices other than our own. Mother Earth and other beings are always communicating with us, but we rarely listen.

Go to the garden, park, or woods. Find a quiet place and sit with your back to a tree. Close your eyes and listen.

Do you hear the insects buzzing? Do you hear the birds singing? Do you hear the wind rustling the trees?

Try to sense the pattern of the lives around you—the insects in the earth, the animals and plants, and their interaction with the sun, the wind, and the rain, thousands of individual lives interacting and living in accord.

Allow yourself to become part of that harmony.

TEA MEDITATION

When you make your morning tea or coffee, inhale the fragrance and acknowledge the gift of the leaves or beans, their growth, harvest, and journey to you, and their effects on your body.

RAISIN MEDITATION

Take a raisin and hold it in your hand. Examine its colour, its shape, all the little wrinkles. Smell it. Imagine how it grew from Mother Earth on the grapevine, absorbing the sun, the wind, and the rain. Imagine its journey to you. Now put it in your mouth and taste its sweetness, the sum product of all these things. Chew it mindfully and with gratitude.

WALKING MEDITATION

As you walk to work or stroll in the park, feel your feet connecting with Mother Earth. Feel her supporting you, nurturing you. If you can take your shoes off, all the better.

DREAMING WITH THE EYES OPEN

When you first arrive at a place, greet it as you would a living being. Stand or sit quietly for a while. Try to relax your body. Still your mind by closing your eyes and concentrating on the sounds around you. Perhaps you can hear the birds and the wind or the rolling of the sea on the shore. Be aware of your mind probing around the area, seeking for its ambience, its energies, and the flow of the sacred within it.

Open your eyes. While maintaining this heightened consciousness, you can walk through the landscape and explore it with new levels of awareness.

THE WITCH WALK

The witch walk is a pilgrimage that relies on the sacred to give you direction. To begin, dedicate the journey to the Gods and ask that you will be guided. Put yourself in the light trance state called dreaming with the eyes open. Now ask the Gods to direct your footsteps, turning right or left as they dictate. Sometimes, you will feel the directions as a magnetic pull, other times as a heat on your face. Sometimes the Gods will send messengers in the form of birds, animals, or butterflies to lead the way. Treat everything that happens to you on a witch walk as significant, whether this is a person or animal you meet, a place or plant you discover, and so on.

Offerings

One of the simplest and most profound things you can do is make offerings to the Gods: flowers, found objects such as special feathers or shells, incense, food, and drink. The Gods don't demand expensive and exotic gifts but appreciate something that has meaning to you.

Offerings are not given with the expectation of receiving something in return; they are not given to pay back the Gods. Offerings are an outward manifestation of your intent for a good relationship with the Gods. Our ancestors believed that the Gods and spirits fed on the essence of the offerings, and this helps us understand their value if we think of them in this way: creating an energetic link between the material and the spiritual.

We offer the Gods the best of what we have. It is important that your offerings are not just what is convenient, but something that takes some thought, time, and effort. A home-baked loaf of bread will mean more than a shop-bought one. A posy of wild or garden flowers you have plucked with intent mean more than a bouquet bought in a garage.

You can offer words of thanks or blessings, offer a prayer or sing a song to the Gods, if you wish. You can have an offering bowl on your altar or on your hearth. Some instances of offerings have already been mentioned in this book.

The important thing is that you offer regularly, and from the heart.

CHAPTER 10

· · · · · · · · · · · · · · · ·

Consecration

Consecrate means "to make sacred." By consecrating something, we separate it from the secular world and dedicate it to the Gods and sacred use. We consecrate the tools and other objects we use in ritual and magic. Until consecration, an object is just an object—a statue, a knife, a cup, a candle, a talisman, and so on. Consecration permanently transforms the essence of that object. After consecration, it becomes a spiritual home for the powers invoked into it, bridging the gap between humans and the Gods. When we consecrate something, we invoke gods and energies to impart conscious magical power into an object and give it purpose. It becomes a living thing, full of the power that is invoked into it. Consecration is an expansion of consciousness of the witch and of the Gods themselves.

How to Consecrate an Object

We consecrate all the things we want to dedicate to sacred work—the place of working or worship, the altar, magical tools, divining instruments, talismans and amulets, statues of the Gods, candles, robes, magical jewellery, and so on—to the service of the divine.

1. Intention

Why do you want to consecrate the object or tool? How do you want to use it? What do you want to achieve with it? Is this tool or object the best way to achieve that goal? How will you consecrate it? You have to be very clear what the intention is and express it unambiguously. Consecration will change the essence of the object.

2. Preparation

Choose the right time to perform the consecration. It is useful to use a time of prime energy: a waxing energy sabbat (Imbolc, Ostara, Beltane, Midsummer), waxing moon, full moon, or noonday. Most tools should not be consecrated at a time of waning energy.

Choose the physical ingredients you need, such as incense, oils, herbs, inscribing tools, symbols, and so on. Each ingredient must be chosen for its inherent properties and magical correspondences to reinforce the intent and the power of the intent.

3. Purification

All tools and objects must be cleansed and purified before consecration to remove any stray or negative energies they may have accumulated from previous owners or the environment they came from (shops, markets, etc.). Before you consecrate a tool, you must be sure it is free of such accretions.

You can perform both a physical and a spiritual cleansing on the objects. They acquire ordinary dirt, and the dirt hangs on to vibrations. Statues and glass objects can be cleaned with soapy water. Cleanse wooden tools and knife handles with a damp cloth and apply wood oil. Leather pouches can be cleansed with leather cleaner.

The spiritual cleansing comes with visualising the tool being cleansed of all negative energy as you wash it with running water, if this won't damage the object. Alternatively, pass it through cleansing incense, such as frankincense or sage or through a candle flame.

Before you begin the ritual, purify yourself. You might take a purification bath or shower, then purify yourself spiritually and emotionally by suspending the thoughts and concerns of everyday life. Banish malice, hate, envy, and negativity from your mind, or these will be imbued into the object.

4. Visualisation

Visualise what you are about to do and what you want it to achieve.

5. INVOCATION

This is the part of the consecration that unites the physical and the spiritual, holds it together, and starts its manifesting in the world. It is done by appealing to the higher forces—the Gods—for help, imbuing the physical anchor (the tool) with what you desire as hard as you can and speaking the words of consecration, all the time concentrating on the desired outcome.

Afterward

This act of consecration binds the tool to you. You should use it as soon as possible to strengthen the energy of the tool. The more you work with the tool and tune in to its purpose, the stronger it will become. A tool left neglected on the shelf will gradually leach power. The more you can use it or even just carry it with you, the stronger it becomes.

Reconsecration

Tools will need to be cleansed and reconsecrated occasionally if other people have handled them, if they have been left unused for a while, or if they have been in negative environments. If you have washed your robe, it should be reconsecrated afterward.

CONSECRATION RITUAL

When we consecrate a tool, we usually do it by the powers of the four elements and dedicate it to the service of the Gods. You will need the following:

> GOD AND GODDESS STATUES OR REPRESENTATIONS
>
> EARTH: BOWL OF SOIL
>
> AIR: INCENSE
>
> FIRE: CANDLE
>
> WATER: BOWL OF WATER

You don't need to cast a circle, but you should invoke sacred space (see page 95) to perform the consecration.

Take your new tool and concentrate on your intent. Focus your awareness on the tool and think about what you want to use it for. Kiss the tool.

Hold the tool with both hands and say,

> *I call upon the Lord and Lady* [or whichever gods/goddesses you wish] *to be with me and witness.*
> *I consecrate this tool in your honour, my Lord and Lady*
> *I make it sacred and put it aside for thy service.*
> *To be used in love.*
> *Lord and Lady, so mote it be.*

Take the item and pass it through the incense:

> *Powers of east and air*
> *I do charge and consecrate this* [wand, athame, whatever it is]
> *And make it sacred.*
> *Lord and Lady, so mote it be.*

Take the item and pass it through the flame of the candle:

> *Powers of south and fire*
> *I do charge and consecrate this* [wand, athame, whatever it is]
> *And make it sacred.*
> *Lord and Lady, so mote it be.*

Take the item and pass it through the water:

> *Powers of west and water*
> *I do charge and consecrate this* [wand, athame, whatever it is]
> *And make it sacred.*
> *Lord and Lady, so mote it be.*

Take the item and touch it to the bowl of earth:

> *Powers of north and earth*
> *I do charge and consecrate this* [wand, athame, whatever it is]
> *And make it sacred.*
> *Lord and Lady, so mote it be.*

Finish by saying,

> Lord and Lady, divine father and mother
> Thank you for being with me this night.
> You have witnessed this consecration of [whatever the tool is]
> That I have set aside in your service.
> I ask that you are with me all my days
> Lighting my path.
> Guide me as I use this [tool] in your honour.
> Blessed be.

CHAPTER 11

· · · · · · · · · · · · · · · · · ·

Creating Sacred Space

Most pagan societies had a tradition of domestic altars, and this survived Christianity in some places. In Slavic homes, for example, the red corner was placed opposite the hearth; this corner had shelves that held sacred icons and pictures of the ancestors and was a place for private worship. Candles and incense were lit in front of it, and it was decorated with embroidered cloths, seasonal flowers, and greenery on special occasions.

An altar is the perfect place to connect with deity, meditate, and make magic. It doesn't have to be a big table covered with an embroidered cloth and permanently set with fancy candlesticks and a chalice. You can use your hearth as an altar or make an altar on a mantle-piece, a shelf, a niche, a windowsill, a low box or table, or even on a tray or in a box you can put away if you don't want anyone else to see it. What you put on your altar is up to you. You could have deity statues, candles, and your magical and divination tools, or you could make it entirely discreet, with stones and natural objects to represent your deities, a candle in a jar and perhaps an incense burner, special objects you have found, seasonal decorations, fresh flowers, an offering bowl, and so on.

Altar Consecration

To dedicate or revitalise the altar, you should consecrate it. Cleanse the altar itself, and each item you place upon it, with purification wash or with a ritual fumigation (page 35) if the objects can't be washed.

Altar cloth

Objects for your altar

Purification wash (page 34)

Frankincense burning on charcoal (on a safe dish)

White candle

Bowl of water

Bowl of earth

Lay the cloth on the altar and add your items in a way that pleases you. Pass the dish of burning frankincense over the altar and say,

I *consecrate you with the powers of air.*

Pass the candle over it and say,

I *consecrate you with the powers of fire.*

Sprinkle a little spring water over the altar and say,

I *consecrate you with the powers of water.*

Hold the earth bowl over the altar and say,

I *consecrate you with the powers of earth. Lord and Lady* [or whichever deities the altar is dedicated to], I *have prepared this altar in your honour. Let blessing be.*

Maintaining Your Altar

Work with it regularly; a neglected altar loses its power. The more you work with it, the more power it accrues. Approach it with reverence. Cleanse it regularly with lustral water (page 34) or frankincense incense at the waning moon. Your altar should be a joy, and not a duty; if it no longer serves its purpose or gives you joy, it is fine to change or remove it.

Connecting the Physical and Spiritual Worlds

To perform ceremony and ritual, we usually begin by creating sacred space where we deliberately leave behind everyday concerns and bring our entire attention to the spiritual.

When you create sacred space, the intention is to create a safe energy field where you can remove yourself from the concerns of the mundane world. Sacred space is the place where the physical and the spiritual connect. It is not necessary to have a permanent altar, temple, or meditation room, travel to an ancient sacred site, or cast a circle every time you want to be in sacred space. When the essence of your being reaches out into the spiritual essence of your environment, you may create it by intent and consecration, wherever you are—in the kitchen, the garden, your hearth or your altar, or just in your imagination by using visualisation.

If you are working indoors, it is always a good idea to physically and spiritually cleanse the space you are going to use. You might ring a bell or use a Tibetan sound bowl to shift stagnant energy. You might use an incense or ritual fumigation.

The Centre

Wherever we are is the centre of the universe for us. Above us is the sky, below us the earth. Then we have the directions of front, back, left, and right, and thus we orientate ourselves. We have to know where we are before we can undertake any journey, including spiritual ones. We begin at the centre, and around that centre, we build sacred space.

For the hearth witch, the hearth may become the centre upon which ritual and magic are performed. The walls of the house become north, south, east, and west. If you are using an altar as the centre, you might place your magical tools on it: the sword or athame of intellect and intent, the cup of emotions and spiritual aspiration, the pentacle of manifestation and crystallisation, and the wand of will and focus. They represent the four mystical elements from which everything is made: air, water, earth, and fire, respectively.

You don't have to use a physical centre if you don't wish to. Remember that your heart is your own sacred centre.

Fivefold Sacred Space

For much of my personal work, to create sacred space, I use a wooden pentacle on my altar with a tealight at each point for the five elements: air (yellow tealight), fire (red tealight), water (blue tealight), earth (green tealight), and spirit (purple tealight).

Light your incense. Call in each element in turn:

> *Guardians of the east,*
> *Airy spirits of the winds*
> *Arise and come unto me*
> *Guardians of the east, hail and welcome.*

Light the yellow candle.

> *Guardians of the south*
> *Burning spirits of the flame*
> *Arise and come unto me*
> *Guardians of the south, hail and welcome.*

Light the red candle.

> *Guardians of the west*
> *Misty spirits of the waters*
> *Arise and come unto me*
> *Guardians of the west, hail and welcome.*

Light the blue candle.

> *Guardians of the north*
> *Elementals of the rich, moist soil*
> *Arise and come unto me*
> *Guardians of the north, hail and welcome.*

Light the green candle.

> *I stand in love upon the Earth Mother*
> *I stand in awe beneath the Sky Father*
> *Lord and Lady*
> *Blessed be.*

Light the purple candle.

Your sacred space is now open. You can go on to perform your ritual.

To close the sacred space when you have finished, put out each candle with these words:

> *Guardians of the east,*
> *Thank you for your presence here tonight*
> *Guardians of the east, hail and farewell.*

Extinguish the yellow candle.

> *Guardians of the south*
> *Thank you for your presence here tonight*
> *Guardians of the south, hail and farewell.*

Extinguish the red candle.

> *Guardians of the west*
> *Thank you for your presence here tonight*
> *Guardians of the west, hail and farewell.*

Extinguish the blue candle.

> *Guardians of the north*
> *Thank you for your presence here tonight*
> *Guardians of the north, hail and farewell.*

Extinguish the green candle.

> *Earth Mother, Sky Father, Lord and Lady*
> *Thank you for your presence here tonight.*
> *It is not for me to bid you be gone.*
> *Instead, I ask that you are with me all my days*
> *Guiding my path.*
> *Lord and Lady, blessed be.*

Extinguish the purple candle.

Sevenfold Sacred Space

Sacred space is created as a mirror of the divine. Traditionally, a more formal creation of sacred space involves calling in the seven directions: centre, above, below, north, south, east, and west.

This is a method of calling in the seven directions by visualisation that you may use if you want to and if it feels suitable. It is not necessary every time you work, and some ceremonies, like the lighting of the fire or candle, do not need it.

Be still, feel yourself fully present where you are, and honour your centre.

Visualise the sky above you and honour Father Sun. You might say, out loud or in your mind, "I honour you, Father Sun," or words that seem suitable to you.

Feel the energy of the sky flowing down through you deep into the earth.

Be aware of the earth beneath you, the seeds and roots buried in the soil, and give honour to Mother Earth out loud or in your mind. You might say, "I honour you, Mother Earth," or words that seem suitable to you.

Turn your attention to the direction of the east, the direction of air, and give honour to the direction of the east out loud or in your mind.

Turn to the direction of the south, the direction of fire, and give honour to the south out loud or in your mind.

Turn to the direction of the west, the direction of water, and give honour to the direction of the west out loud or in your mind.

Turn to the direction of the north, the direction of earth, and give honour to the direction of the north out loud or in your mind.

Your sacred space is now open. You can go on to perform your ritual.

Once your work is complete, the sacred space should be closed.

Visualise the sky above you, thank Father Sun, and release the energy with gratitude.

Think of the earth beneath you, thank Mother Earth, and release the energy with gratitude.

Turn to the direction of the east and release the energy with gratitude.

Turn to the direction of the south and release the energy with gratitude.

Turn to the direction of the west and release the energy with gratitude.

Turn to the direction of the north and release the energy with gratitude.

Place your hands over your heart and give thanks for your centre.

Casting a Circle

Though I rarely cast and consecrate a circle for personal work and rituals, I do cast a circle for more formal group rituals as it draws everyone's intentions together. Like other creations of hallowed space, a cast circle aims to re-create the macrocosm in microcosm. It connects to the powers of above and below and opens the gateways to the powers of north, south, east, and west so that they may flow in, meeting at the centre. It is strictly built step-by-step and consecrated at each stage. The cast and consecrated circle amplifies the power raised within it.

To begin, we honour spirits of place as well as the spirits of the ward that protect the land. We invite them to come to our circle and join in our celebrations.

At the beginning of ritual, the cosmic axis is drawn through the centre of the ring from the heavens above, through the hearth fire, and down into the underworld, and thus we are linked to all three realms so that we are truly between the worlds.

The next act is to define the ritual area by drawing a circle around the boundaries of the ring. This marks it out as consecrated space, a place where Gods and humans can communicate, where the mundane meets the sacred.

Next, we open the gateways to the elemental powers of the east, south, west, and north, so that they may flow into the ring to meet at the centre of the circle, where all times and all places are one, and all are accessible.

Go to the east and say,

> Airy spirits of the winds
> Gentle breath of the dawn
> Arise and come unto me this night.

Travel around the ring to the south and say,

> Burning spirits of the flame
> Transforming as you devour
> Arise and come unto me this night.

Travel around the ring to the west and say,

> Misty spirits of the waters
> Haunters of the twilight pools
> Arise and come unto me this night.

Travel around the ring to the north and say,

> *Elementals of the rich, moist soil*
> *Earth spirits of rock, stone, and crystal*
> *Arise and come unto me this night.*

The next stage of the ritual is to invoke the Gods themselves and open a channel to the higher powers. Then a statement of intent is made outlining the purpose of the ritual. After this, the body of the ritual is performed. Every part of the ritual should flow naturally to the next without any awkward pauses and loss of focus.

When all is finished, the circle is dissolved. The beings who have attended are thanked for their help. They are offered a blessing before they depart. Closing the rite properly is as important as opening it correctly. Take the knife and cut through the cosmic axis, then go to the boundary of the circle near the east and say words to the effect of,

> *Mighty powers of the east, thank you for guarding our circle and for witnessing our*
> *rites. I bless you in the name of the Lord and the Lady* [or whatever deities you call
> upon].

Repeat in all the other directions.
Then the Gods are thanked with words such as,

> *It is not for us to bid those whom we worship to be gone. Instead, we ask that they are*
> *with us all our days, lighting our paths and guiding our feet. Blessed be.*

Finally, it is important to make a definite end to the ritual with the words,

> *This rite is ended. Blessed be.*

Put out the candles and dismantle the ritual space.

CHAPTER 12

. . . .

Ritual

If prayer is talking to the Gods, and meditation is listening for the Gods, ritual is a dialogue where communication goes both ways; ritual brings us and the Gods together.

The aim of every ritual is to align the sacred and the mundane, to allow the greater forces of the cosmos to flow, reforging the links between you and the Gods. Each ritual you perform will progressively make that connection easier and more permanent, deeper and more transcendent.

Rituals can be simple or complex. You can have a big ritual with a cast circle, long rhyming speeches, and a plethora of tools and paraphernalia, and sometimes that is the right thing to do. However, overly elaborate ceremonies can become nothing more than theatrical performances. If you are more focused on fancy robes, wands with expensive crystals on, and complicated scripts, you can lose sight of the sacred intent of what you are doing. You must be fully present and work with intent, only using words and actions that harmonise you with nature's patterns and serve the intent of the ritual. It doesn't matter how poetic the words or how fancy the robes you wear are; without intent, you haven't performed sacred ritual at all, but acted in an empty pantomime. Indeed, you might find that your most profound connections come from simple acts that come directly from the heart; you can connect to the sacred through small things, as well as through the big things.

When you give thanks, when you make offerings to your deities, when you bless your seeds or open your heart to the spirit of place, this too is ritual.

An effective ritual does not blindly follow a set text or act from habit, but sensitively and mindfully does what will harmonise you with the rhythms around you in that moment—it strives to do the right thing at the right time. This means being sensitive to the energies around you, to the cycles of the moon and year. Your desires are one thing, but they won't override what is happening around you.

Remember that this is a two-way exchange. Don't just charge in and make demands of the Gods without listening to the other side of the interchange. If you were having an important conversation with a friend but rushed in to change the subject before they had finished speaking, your friend would probably be irritated with you. If you tried to dominate the conversation entirely, didn't listen to anything they said, and just talked about yourself, they would definitely be annoyed with you and the friendship might well be at an end. If you do this in a ritual exchange with the Gods, they will likely avoid working with you again.

Wherever you choose to work ritual, you need to be sensitive to the web of energies of the place where you are working, whether this is your home, your garden, or a woodland grove. It takes time to do this and to build up a relationship with its inhabitants, visible and invisible, in a respectful way that fosters trust. Imagine if you were to barge into a stranger's house, light a cigarette, help yourself to the contents of the fridge, and demand the inhabitants serve you when they don't know you from Adam. You wouldn't do it in the mundane world, and the same applies to the places we work ritual.

The Steps of Ritual

The steps can be simple for a small personal ritual, or they can be elaborated on for a larger group ritual, but increased complexity doesn't necessarily mean greater effectiveness. The basic steps of ritual are as follows:

1. Intent. Knowing what you want the ritual to achieve.

2. Preparation. Designing the ritual to fit its intent (words, symbols, time, place, etc.) to create a harmonic resonance that amplifies that intent. Next is the cultivation of a positive state of mind; you must believe you can and will succeed. Before you begin,

make sure you have everything ready that will be needed in the work ahead. Purify yourself.

3. Invocation. A true ritual is more than a performance that mentally stimulates the participants with theatre; it opens a channel to the higher powers. It creates sacred space and invokes outside forces to aid us in our work.

4. The body of the ritual is performed. The performance of a ritual brings it to life, bridging the gap between us and the Gods. Speaking its words fills them with power.

5. Thanking the spirits involved. The beings who have attended are thanked for their help. They are offered a blessing before they depart.

6. Closing. This is as important as opening correctly. If you feel ill or unusually tired after a ritual, you have not done something right. If you don't close the power down, particularly if you are working in your own home, it will cause problems that may manifest in the form of odd noises, balls of light, smells, a disturbed atmosphere, and so on.

If Your Practice No Longer Serves You

Though it is important that you persist in your practice and work through failures, there may come a point where you realise what you are doing just isn't working. When a particular practice has just become an onerous duty, you might need to rethink your methods, as this is not honouring the Gods or fostering your spiritual development. Ask yourself whether you are trying to do too much and perform too many ceremonies. Go back to what has worked for you in the past and try to reconnect with why you are doing this in the first place.

Myths of the Gods

When we create rituals, we appeal to particular gods and spirits. We may employ the myths of the Gods in that creation.

Humans have always sought to understand their existence and explain their connection to the world and the divine through myths. Every culture has its own collection of stories and legends, gods and folklore, handed down from generation to generation in the form of rituals and oral traditions. Myths are not meant to be taken literally, but the reappearance of certain themes, time and again in different mythologies, leads to the realization that these themes portray universal and eternal truths. They serve as metaphors for an inexpressible transcendence and show us what shape the universe is, but in such a way that the mystery comes through. They show us our place in the cosmos, on earth, in our tribes and communities. They teach us about ourselves and others and are the keys to understanding the whole of human experience.

The old myths are beautiful and rich with meaning. They are sacred and awe inspiring. They show us a world in which everything is alive, the divine flowing through it, a unified whole. They show us a truth that we cannot challenge or change without diminishing ourselves: we are not separate from nature, or above it, but part of it. They tell of community, connection, compassion, and a deep, embodied sense of belonging to this beautiful living earth.

Gods of Wisdom Ritual

This is a ritual to connect with the gods and goddesses of wisdom. Perform it when you need clear insight into the path ahead. You may already honour a wisdom deity from your tradition, whether this be Athene (Greek), Brighid (Celtic), Ogma (Celtic), Sophia (Gnostic), Odin (Norse), or another. If this is your first time approaching such a deity, proceed with reverence and humility.

You will need the following:

> Rosemary sprigs tied in a bundle with wool
>
> Dish of fresh water
>
> Olive oil
>
> Bread
>
> Cup of wine or fruit juice
>
> White candle
>
> Statue or depiction of your chosen god or goddess

Begin by creating your sacred space. Dip the bundle of rosemary into the fresh clean water and sprinkle the water about the ritual space and yourself. Anoint the candle with the oil, light it, and say,

> [God/goddess name], *god(dess) of wisdom. I come to honour you and make offerings.*
> *Hail [god/goddess name]!*
> *Sacred god(dess) of wisdom*
> *Bringer of clarity and strategy*
> *Bringer of divine justice*
> *I invoke you!*
> *God(dess) of reason and writing*
> *I invoke you.*

Bless the bread, the wine, and the dish of oil and lay it before the depiction/statue of the god/goddess. Dip your fingers in the olive oil, anoint the image, and say,

> [God/goddess name], *I anoint you with oil as an act of devotion and offer you bread and wine.*
> *I pray to you, learned one, clever one*
> *Yours are the gifts of intellect, judgement, reason, and clear vision,*
> *Let them flow within me.*
> *Grant me insight*
> *Show me the path ahead.*

Drink a sip of wine and say,

> *As I drink, may I partake of your ancient knowledge.*

Eat a piece of bread and say,

> *As I eat, may I grow in wisdom.*

Then sit in silent meditation and accept any insight that is given to you. You can use divination with tarot, ogham, or runes to give you further guidance. When you have your answer and are ready to close, say,

> *Wise, strong, powerful, and kind [god/goddess name].*
> *Let your balance between strength and compassion guide me.*
> *Guide me with your wisdom.*
> *Though this rite is ended, I pray that you are with me always.*
> *Blessed be.*

Put out the candle. Close your sacred space.

Put the leftover bread outside and pour the wine on the earth as a libation to the god/goddess.

Father Sun Ritual

Father Sun governs the pattern of life; his cycles divide the hours, days, months, and years and the seasonal round of sowing, growth, harvest, and decay. Before he was set spinning on his course, there was only chaos; it is only the movement of the sun that makes life possible.

We depend on the relationship of Mother Earth and Father Sun for life; in the summer, the long hours of daylight and warmth make the crops grow, but in the winter darkness and cold, they shrivel and die.

Just as Father Sun governs the cycle of the year, he governs the magical tides of the day. From where we stand on earth, each day the sun seems to rise in the east, scattering the powers of darkness and diffusing light and fertility as he climbs to his zenith at noon. Then he declines, descending into the west and eventually sinking below the horizon, only to return with the following dawn. Each sunrise demonstrates the victory of life over the forces of death and darkness; it is a metaphor for our spiritual and physical life, reflecting our own experiences of birth, growth, decay, and death, as well as our hope of rebirth, our struggles against negativity and the triumph of spirit. For our ancestors, the eternal cycle of the sun was the central paradigm of their spiritual beliefs.

As Father Sun travels across the sky, he sees everything that happens on earth and uncovers those secrets hidden by darkness, freeing people from illusion. He battles the forces of negativity and fills all things with a spiritual light. He coaxes the seed from the barren winter earth. He melts away fear just as he melts away the morning mist. Father Sun is a power greater than any individual life; he represents eternal truth, justice, and enlightenment. The energy of the sun is creation on all levels, abundance, courage, health, joy—life-giving, truthful, invigorating, harmonising.

Gather the following.

> 6 YELLOW OR GOLD CANDLES
>
> SYMBOLS SUCH AS WHEELS, SUN MASKS, AND SPIRALS
>
> FRANKINCENSE

Create your sacred space. Light the candles and the incense. Say,

> *Father Sun, I call to you.*
> *You are the bright and shining light*

You are the eye of the sky

You see right through to the limits of the darkness.

You behold everything, even into the realm of chaos.

Your blessings fall upon the earth and cause the crops to grow.

Father Sun, I invoke you.

Wait until you feel the presence of the god. Pause to experience this, then say,

Father Sun

You are the radiant energy that brings forth life.

You banish all shadows

You are all truth.

You inspire us through prophecy

You inspire us with music and poetry

You inspire us with spiritual yearning.

Each dawn, you give us a vision of life renewed.

Father Sun, be with me and renew me.

Imagine a golden radiance coming down from the sun, enfolding you in a glowing light that penetrates every cell of your being, invigorating and renewing your body and spirit. It flows with love, joy, and beauty; it flows with truth. Enjoy this for as long as you wish.

When you have finished, say,

Father Sun

May your divine flame of inspiration be kindled within me.

May my eyes be opened to all the joy in the world.

Father Sun, I give thanks for your gifts.

You light my path and give me life.

Be with me always.

This rite is ended. Blessed be.

Put out the candles. Close your sacred space.

Mother Earth Ritual

Mother Earth is one of the most important aspects of divinity we honour, because she supports us and nurtures us. Without her, we have nothing. As well as providing shelter, food, medicine, and all that is necessary for life, she is the basis of our spiritual existence here on earth. She has had many names in different parts of the world: some call her Gaia and others Rhea or Cybele, while to many she is simply known as the mother, because she is the bringer of fertility and presides over the whole cycle of being: planting, growth, and harvest; birth, growth, decline, death, and rebirth.

She is the great matrix of nature, and her spirit flows throughout it, connecting it into a unified, sacred whole. Her magic flows throughout the world. All space is sacred space because it is her body.

We are all children of Mother Earth: animals, plants, people, rocks, streams, oceans.

Invoke your sacred space.

Light a green candle on your altar and say,

> *Mother Earth, I call to you.*
>
> *You are all life; you are all abundance.*
>
> *You produce everything in nature; you produced me, your child.*
>
> *You are first in all things, you surround me.*
>
> *You are beneath my feet.*
>
> *You give me the food I eat, the water I drink.*
>
> *From you comes all I see, all that breathes.*
>
> *Mother Earth, I invoke you.*

Wait until you feel the presence of the goddess. Pause to experience this, then say,

> *Mother Earth*
>
> *Your vital force flows throughout the world*
>
> *Pushing up with every shoot*
>
> *Each fledgling bird*
>
> *Each opening flower.*
>
> *You are the life-giver*
>
> *The woman of power*
>
> *Who rejuvenates the earth.*
>
> *Flow through me too*
>
> *And let me know your touch.*

Imagine a green energy flowing up from beneath the earth, nurturing, loving, energising. It surrounds you and flows through you and all things. Experience the connection for as long as you wish, then say,

Mother Earth

You are the bringer of fertility

You are the great matrix of nature

Your spirit flows throughout it

Connecting it into a unified, sacred whole.

You are the mother of all living

And your love is poured out upon the earth.

You are the all-encompassing source of life.

Within you, there is no separation, no judgement

All life, all creation is sacred.

Your nurturing flow of life is always available

For I am your own child.

Bless me, mother.

Finish the ritual by saying,

Mother Earth, I honour you and all your creation. Blessed be.

Reflect on this for a while. Put out the candle.

Close your sacred space.

GODDESS OF JUSTICE RITUAL

The heavenly scales of the constellation Libra belong to the goddesses of justice. In Greece, she was Themis, who personified *themis*, the natural law that comes from the Gods, as opposed to *nomoi*, the laws created by men. She was represented with scales in one hand and a sword or cornucopia in the other. Her justice is not human-made but is the maintenance of cosmic balance.

Sometimes we need to take stock and examine what it is in our lives, and in the world around us, that has slipped out of balance, and strive to return it to equilibrium. Where we have strayed, we must bring ourselves back to the path.

Gather the following.

BLUE CANDLE

SET OF BALANCING SCALES

SEVERAL SMALL PIECES OF PAPER

PEN

Meditate on what you need to bring back into harmony and what you need to make atonement for. This can be personal or global.

Write down each thing you need to bring back into harmony on a separate piece of paper and place them on one side of the scale.

Write down the atonements you can make (or the world can make) for each transgression and set them on the other side of the scale. The idea is to get them to balance.

Invoke your sacred space. Light the candle and say,

> *Goddess of justice and divine law.*
> *I invoke you.*
> *Daughter of the stars, you who holds the scales of balance*
> *I call to you for justice.*
> *I call upon you to witness my words*
> *And help me bring about balance.*
> *So mote it be.*

Allow the candle to burn itself out. Put the pieces of paper in a box and keep them on your altar (or somewhere safe) until next year, when you can take them out and read them and see what has changed before burning them and performing this ritual again with new concerns.

GODDESS OF LOVE RITUAL

Set the altar with the following.

> STATUE OF LOVE GODDESS
>
> OFFERING BOWL
>
> ROSE OIL
>
> HONEY OR HONEY SUBSTITUTE
>
> OLIVE OIL
>
> INCENSE BURNER
>
> INCENSE
>
> 7 GREEN CANDLES
>
> VASE OF ROSES
>
> BELL

Set up your sacred space. Light the candles. Ring the bell seven times. Say,

> Goddess of love
>
> Morning star and evening star.
>
> You who are tenderness and compassion
>
> You who are fury and strength
>
> You who walk the line between the sacred and the profane
>
> I call to you.
>
> Goddess of love
>
> You join the world with harmony.
>
> For all things spring from love.
>
> Illustrious, laughter-loving queen
>
> You delight in acts of pleasure and mirth.
>
> I call upon you with reverence to seek your gifts.

Light the incense and say,

> Hear me, goddess of love! Heavenly, laughter-loving queen. I ask that you fill my life with joy. May this offering please you.

Anoint the statue with rose oil and say,

> Hear us, goddess of love! Goddess of love and compassion, I ask that you fill my life with love. May this offering please you.

Anoint yourself with rose oil. Pour olive oil into the offering bowl and say,

> Hear me, goddess of love! Goddess from which all things spring. I ask that you fill my life with emotional nourishment. May this offering please you.

Taste the olive oil. Pour honey into the offering bowl and say,

> Hear me goddess of love. Joyous queen. I ask that you fill my life with your sweetness. May this offering please you.

Taste the honey and say,

> Goddess of love, your touch fills our souls with fire, and none can resist your power. The power of love makes us feel more alive and that everything is sharper in focus, every colour brighter, and every sound more beautiful. The very first divine being who emerged from primordial chaos—and the whole driving force behind creation—is love, which binds spirit and matter together, creating the world from opposites.

Love is the inner harmony that brings us closer to the oneness that is union with the divine.

Spend some time meditating on this. Ring the bell once. Say,

Goddess of love
Open my spirit to joy and my heart to love.
Bless me with compassion and kindness
Let your goodness flow through me.
Surround me with love.
Let love flow to all beings.
Far-shining goddess
Hold us in your loving embrace.
Blessed be.

Ring the bell seven times. Finish by saying,

It is not for me to bid she whom I worship to be gone. Instead, I ask that the goddess of love is with me all my days, filling my heart with joy and compassion. This rite is ended, blessed be.

Put out the candles and close your sacred space.

Part Four
Natural Cycles

I will tell you the story of the love between Father Sun and Mother Earth, and about how their devotion makes all life on earth possible.

Like all lovers, their relationship has its cycles, sometimes close and passionate, sometimes cold and distant.

In spring, the youthful Sun casts his golden gaze upon the Earth, and she stirs in response to his gentle caresses and begins to blossom.

As summer comes, their love becomes hot and passionate, and they spend long hours locked in an ardent embrace. He is strong and virile. She is at her most beautiful, lush and in full bloom.

But as autumn comes, the Sun increasingly feels age come upon him, and lacking the vigour of his prime, he visits less each day. She gives her attention to the harvest she has birthed, the fruit and the grain.

Eventually, the Sun grows so old and weak, he barely appears, and winter comes. Deprived of her lover's light and warmth, the Earth loses her own ripe beauty; the leaves on the trees fall, and plants shrivel. She withdraws into herself, shrinking into the crone's white cloak of snow as she watches her lover decline toward his death.

But she has a secret—she knows that at the winter solstice, when all seems lost and destined to descend forever into darkness and chaos, she will bring him to rebirth, and the cycle will begin again.

This is the story of the eternal return.

· · · · · · · · · · ·

One of the most important aspects of our path is learning to work with natural cycles. In the modern world, we are dominated by the clock and by the calendar, but these are artificial constructs, part of the stresses and obligations of contemporary life. The earth, the sun, the moon, and the whole of nature works to different cycles.

Only a couple of hundred years ago, most people wouldn't have had access to clocks; they rose with the sun and went to bed when it set. Today, we probably wake with the alarm, and go to bed at a specific time, and have to perform the same job all year round, though we are surprised to find that we don't have the same daily levels of wakefulness and performance summer and winter alike. This is because our bodies have evolved to respond to the physical cycles of light and dark. Physically and spiritually, we are intrinsically linked to nature's phases, even though we might not be aware of it.

Nature has its own rhythms. The sun rises and sets; the moon waxes, grows to pregnant fullness, and wanes again. Energy pours into the world during spring and summer, making the earth blossom, reaches its zenith at the summer solstice, and pours out again during the autumn and winter, when Mother Nature draws everything back into herself.

To make our magic, we must recognise that there are rhythms and patterns everywhere. We time our rituals and their intentions accordingly and attempt to harmonise our work with them—we don't make magic of growth when the tides are ebbing, and we don't perform rituals of banishment when the tides are swelling. Nature tells us that there is a moment to act, to perform a specific ritual or act of magic, that will never come again. Before it has come or when it has passed, we must be still, or we will create only disharmony.

The calendar won't tell you when the right time comes to perform a ritual—the sun, the moon, the stars, the trees, and the wind will tell you. There is a time for planting, when the season and the weather provide the perfect conditions, a moment when a flower or an herb is in perfect condition to pick, and so it is with magic.

CHAPTER 13

. . . .

The Cycle of the Year

Tuning in to the wheel of the year means being absorbed into the whole year, not just the eight sabbats, and developing a deep awareness of its ever-changing energy tides. Depending on where you live, these may be obvious or subtle. Here in England, we have four very distinct seasons. In spring, a great flood of energy pours into the land, waking it up; green shoots push their way through the earth, birds and mammals become more active and start to mate. Then summer brings a time of flowering lushness and full growth, but in autumn, things start to slow down again as the great tide of energy recedes, and the leaves fall. In the cold dark days of winter, the land falls asleep, holding close the fallen seeds until spring returns. It is important to work with the tides of energy where you are, which may be very different. I was in Malaysia recently, where I was told they only have two seasons: hot and hotter. It's pretty obvious that I would have to adjust my practices if I lived there!

Embracing the wheel of the year means putting aside your books and your screens to get out there and experience nature in its entirety: summer and winter, rain and shine, heat and cold. Away from all our twenty-first century distractions, we can begin to make real and profound spiritual connections.

The Hearth Witch's Year

The hearth witch's year is a cycle of seasonal activities and celebrations.

During the soft days of spring, when warmth and life return, we begin work on the garden, tilling the soil and planting our seeds. We go out to collect nature's first wild medicines: nettles, chickweed, cleavers, tonics that feed and purify the body after its winter sluggishness. We make the magic of beginnings, things that will come to completion in the fullness of time.

In the hot bright days of summer, we tend our gardens, weeding and hoeing, harvesting the first salad and fruit crops, a wealth of fresh food. We collect our herbs at the peak of their growth and turn them into teas, tinctures, and salves, or set them to dry to make remedies to see us through the year. We make the magic of expansion, of growth, of union.

Then comes the abundant bounty of autumn, when all the work on the land pays off and we get busy preserving it, freezing and canning, making jams and wines. The hedgerows are full of wild fruit and nuts, so we collect and make use of these gifts too. We prepare our homes for the winter ahead. We make magic of protection and warding.

Finally come the frozen days of winter, when Mother Nature draws all into herself and rests. We cleave to our hearth fire and turn our attention to indoor activities. We make the magic of dreaming, of deep connection, of drawing ourselves into our roots to reconnect with our deepest selves.

Then the year, at Yule, begins anew with the rebirth of the sun, and the whole cycle starts again, never the same twice, but a continuing cycle nonetheless. The magic and rituals we celebrate throughout the year reflect this cycle.

Ancient pagans had many, many festivals throughout the entire year, which marked the seasonal tides and the solar, agricultural, and pastoral cycles. On a daily, weekly, and monthly basis, we can celebrate the ebb and flow of the natural cycles with smaller, personal rituals, just as our ancestors did (for more on this, see my *Hearth Witch's Year*).

In this way, we may connect with the great circle of being.

Tuning In to the Cycle of the Year

If you are lucky enough to have a garden, you already have an intimate link with the seasons. If you live in a city, it is even more important to get outside into the natural world; it will benefit your physical and mental health as well as your spiritual practice. Choose a path you can walk on a regular basis, perhaps through a park or public garden, and notice the changes each time you visit. Don't let the weather put you off: the wind and the snow are Mother Nature's gifts too. Use all your senses, not just sight, but listen and smell, feel the textures, and you can even taste if you are sure it is safe (don't take any risks). Sit beneath a tree; become aware of its strength behind your back, its roots deep into the earth, and the rustling of its branches. Be still and open yourself to what is going on around you.

The more you notice, the better. Get a pretty notebook and keep a nature journal. Record when buds start to unfold on particular plants, when they start to flower, and when the seeds form. Notice which trees lose their leaves in winter and which don't, which plants thrive in the winter and which die down. Record the weather, the days of sunshine, windy days, the first frost, and notice how this affects things. Note the first song of the birds in spring, their winter migrations, and the activity of wild animals—when the frogs return to the ponds and when the first bees and butterflies visit. You can press flowers and leaves into your journal or add your photographs and drawings. Year by year, you'll notice that things don't happen on the same day, week, or even month each time, and that sometimes the season seems late. Nature doesn't follow a written calendar but is affected by many factors. You'll soon observe that all life is dependent on the cycle of the sun, the hours of light increasing and decreasing, and the consequent increasing and decreasing warmth of the seasons. The significant points of the solar year are celebrated at the equinoxes and solstices, and these will become even more resonant for you when you celebrate them.

If you have children, you could collect leaves, flowers, pinecones, feathers, twigs, mosses, and acorns each month and make a nature table. I suspect many of us did this in primary school, and it is a lovely way to introduce children to the gifts of each season. We adults can use the natural objects we collect to place on our altars or make decorations, wreaths, corn dollies, nature prints, and other crafts.

If you live somewhere you can forage for wild food, this is a wonderful way to connect with the time of year—collecting fresh salad leaves in spring, blossoms and berries in summer, fruits, nuts, and seeds in autumn. Even in winter there are treasures to be found.

Go on a course or get a knowledgeable friend to guide you, so you are sure that what you are collecting is actually edible and not poisonous.

Notice the weeds in your yard or street. These maligned plants are often very valuable wild food and medicine. Try learning what each one can do, and how it is used. Don't try to discover everything at once, but work with one plant at a time, and really get to know it throughout the year.

Try eating only seasonal foods. This means buying local foods grown in your own regional environment. Being able to eat strawberries all year might seem like a great thing, but they have to be flown in from greenhouses around the world at a high cost to the climate and planet. I only eat my homegrown strawberries in the summer, and can well do without the giant, tasteless supermarket ones in winter. It's a treat I look forward to, along with all the other goodies that only come once a year.

The Four Seasons

Astronomical seasons use the solstices and equinoxes to divide the year, with spring beginning on the vernal equinox, summer on the summer solstice, autumn on the autumn equinox, and winter at the winter solstice. On the other hand, the meteorological seasons (in the northern hemisphere) are based on the annual temperature cycle, so spring will always start on March 1, summer on June 1, autumn on September 1, and winter on December 1. But we witches use the old ways. The old names of the festivals of Midsummer, June 21 (in the northern hemisphere), and Midwinter, December 21 (in the northern hemisphere), tell us our ancestors counted the divisions of the year in quite a different way, according to the light of the sun. The days of greatest darkness fall from Samhain to Imbolc, with Yule at the midpoint, giving us a solar winter. The days of greatest light fall from Beltane to Lughnasa, with the summer solstice at midpoint, giving us a solar summer; the old song tells us "summer is a-comin' in" on May Day, or Beltane. The Irish call Lughnasa the first day of autumn. The Craft defines the seasons as follows, which draws on the old ways of counting the year and reflects the relationship of Father Sun and Mother Earth:

WINTER: Samhain to Imbolc Eve

SPRING: Imbolc to Beltane Eve

SUMMER: Beltane to Lughnasa Eve

AUTUMN: Lughnasa to Samhain Eve

CHAPTER 14

• • • • • • • • • • • • • •

The Eight Sabbats

Most modern pagans celebrate eight sabbats during the course of each year. Each of these sabbats has ancient antecedents, and each one has equal weight in the wheel of the year, and each one has great power.

The solstices and equinoxes are the festivals of the Father Sun, whose light and strength govern and mobilise the whole wheel of the year.

YULE, THE WINTER SOLSTICE: at Yule, the darkest time of year, the sun is reborn as the child of promise, bringing with him the hope that he will grow in strength and return life to the land and that life on earth will continue.

OSTARA, THE VERNAL EQUINOX: the sun has grown in strength and enters his youthful manhood. He courts the maiden earth.

MIDSUMMER, THE SUMMER SOLSTICE: the sun is at the peak of his strength, hot and vigorous, pouring out his energy onto Mother Earth, impregnating her with the coming harvest.

HERFEST, THE AUTUMN EQUINOX: the power of the sun begins to decline with age, cold comes, and he dwindles toward his death on the eve of Yule.

Mother Earth is the source of all we have. The cycle of Mother Earth and harvest is influenced by the light of Father Sun and the consequent light levels and seasonal temperatures. The four great turning points of the earth and harvest cycle are the sabbats of Imbolc, Beltane, Lughnasa, and Samhain, marking when one season pivots into the next, so they are sometimes called the hinges of the year.

IMBOLC: responding to the increasing light, the earth goddess regenerates as maiden and the land begins to stir. This is the traditional beginning of spring.

BELTANE: Mother Earth mates with Father Sun, and the flowering land responds to their love. This is the traditional beginning of summer.

LUGHNASA: the mating of the sun and earth bears fruit, and we begin to harvest the crops. This is the traditional beginning of autumn.

SAMHAIN: as the sun withdraws, the goddess becomes the crone of winter. Plants shrivel. This is the traditional beginning of winter.

Together, the two sets of sabbats celebrate the annual dance of Father Sun and Mother Earth, divinity manifest.

Imbolc

The increasing light of Father Sun is making things happen. After Mother Earth's winter period of rest, a new tide of energy is emerging; we call it the *quickening*, which means "to come to life." All around us we see the first small signs of spring: seeds are stirring in the earth, shoots are uncoiling, sap is rising, the first new lambs are born, and hibernating animals venture out to test the weather. The crone of winter is transforming into the maiden goddess of spring before our eyes.

Mother Nature is our teacher, and she shows us our own powers of regeneration, our ability to renew ourselves time and time again, to rise and grow after fallow periods. We too may rise on the tide of energy that flows at Imbolc. We cleanse and purify ourselves, leaving behind the sloth of winter and all that no longer serves us so that we may be ready to begin the work of the year with a clean slate. We light fires and candles and honour the hearth goddess. We absorb the divine fire into ourselves and allow it to kindle our physical energy, spark our passion for life, and enlighten our spirits.

We celebrate Imbolc as the feast of Brighid, the maid of spring and Celtic goddess of the hearth, healing fire, and creative and poetic inspiration, the "fire in the head" that comes from the Gods. She is the life force that surges throughout creation.

THEMES OF IMBOLC

- Increasing light—Father Sun grows into a youth

- Renewal of the goddess—the crone becomes the maiden

- Regeneration of the land and wakening the earth

- Renewal of fertility with the birth of lambs and growth in plants

- Returning to work on the land after the winter lull

- Emerging from winter introspection

- Transformation

- Purification, cleansing

- Hearth fire

- Creative fire

- Healing fire

- How do you use the three fires of Brighid?

- Creating positive intent for the future (witness the beginning of your own transformation; this is a good time to begin a new diet or exercise programme, for example)

TRADITIONAL FOODS

In the northern regions, where this festival originates, snow often covers the ground and there is little fresh food to be found. Our ancestors would have been using up their stored produce and root vegetables, so the recipes of Imbolc mostly reflect this, but they might have been lucky enough to find some early spring greens, and any young edible shoots are good at this time to remind us that the earth is about to bud. One of the most important themes of Imbolc is the birth of spring lambs—a promise of what is to come—and the consequent lactating of sheep, so if you can and your diet allows it, include some dairy produce in your feast, especially sheep milk and cheese.

TRADITIONAL CRAFTS AND ACTIVITIES

- Burning the last of the Yule evergreen decorations to signify the banishing of winter.

- Burning candles, bonfires, and lanterns to turn back the dark and encourage the sun.

- Crafting Brighid dolls and Brighid's crosses.

- Rites of purification, spring-cleaning, decluttering.

- Cleaning and blessing the garden tools.

SYMBOLS

The hearth, fire, candles, Brighid doll, white quartz crystals, Brighid's crosses, sun wheels, lights, spring flowers and greenery.

MAGICAL HERBS

Alder, benzoin, birch, chickweed, fir, frankincense, heather, rowan, snowdrop, tansy, willow.

Personal Imbolc Ritual

You will need:

BESOM

BOWL OR CAULDRON OF WATER

WHITE CANDLE

3 RED CANDLES

Invoke your sacred space.

Using your besom, sweep and cleanse your sacred space, saying,

I *banish winter*
I *banish winter*
I *banish winter.*

Wash in the water. As you wash, visualise leaving behind all that impedes you in the water. Say,

May I be cleansed and purified of all that hinders me, ready to greet the maiden of spring and the coming year.

Light the white altar candle.

> *In the darkness of the earth, the seeds are stirring;*
> *In the cold of winter, life is quickening.*
> *The goddess wakes from her winter dreaming*
> *And comes to us as the maiden of spring.*
> *Come, Brighid, come and bring your fire.*

Light the first red candle and say,

> *The fire of the hearth warms and comforts. Lady, bless my hearth and home.*

Reflect on how you will use the gifts of the hearth fire. Light the second red candle and say,

> *Let the fire of healing burn within me. Lady, bless me with healing.*

Visualise the fire of healing flowing through you. Reflect on how you will use the gift of healing fire. Light the third red candle and say,

> *Let the fire of inspiration illuminate me. Lady, bless me with inspiration.*

Spend some time in quiet meditation to allow the gift of inspiration to be with you. When you are ready, say,

> *Brighid, goddess of the hearth fire that warms*
> *Goddess of healing fire that restores vitality*
> *Goddess of inspiration and enlightenment*
> *Thank you for being with me this night*
> *And I pray that you are with me always.*
> *Blessed be.*

Reflect on this. When you are ready, say,

> *The rite is ended. Blessed be.*

Close your sacred space. Allow the candles to burn out. Empty the bowl of water onto the earth.

Ostara, the Vernal Equinox

Day by day, Father Sun has been gaining strength. The vernal equinox is a moment of balance, when day and night stand at equal length, but it is a tipping point, and from now on the light will overcome the darkness, and the days will become longer than the nights. The Saxons called March *Lentmonat*, meaning "lengthening" (of the days).

The natural world is invigorated and rejuvenated by this greater light. Mother Earth is wreathed in spring flowers. Birds are nesting, animals are mating, life and fertility are renewed. The maiden goddess begins her courtship with the youthful god.

We can really feel spring in the air and sense its vital energy coursing through our veins with a resurgence of hope. Mother Nature teaches us that we can take the lessons of our fallow periods and sow the seeds of new projects and spiritual growth with the lively expansion of spring.

THEMES OF OSTARA

- The balance of light and darkness, the light gaining

- The strengthening sun

- Renewal, resurgence

- Fertility, life, vigour

- Animal mating

- Nest building and egg laying

- Youth, virility, freshness

- Fresh greenery, flowers

- Maiden goddess, youthful god

- The Green Man, the emergence of the vegetation god

- What seeds will you sow in your garden and in your life?

TRADITIONAL FOODS

With Ostara comes the real arrival of spring. Fresh leaves green the trees, new vegetation covers the land, and flowers are abundant. The sacred foods of Ostara reflect the theme of the renewal of the sun and vegetation god and the beginning of the light half of the year. At the equinox the old breeds of hens began to lay again, triggered by the increasing hours of daylight, and wild birds are mating and building nests. The egg is a symbol of new life. Include some eggs in your feast, if your diet allows, or if you are vegan, make a centrepiece of decorated papier-mâché eggs to reflect this theme. Hot cross buns are marked with a cross, originally a solar symbol of the solstices and equinoxes. Simnel cake is traditional, with thirteen balls of marzipan on top for the thirteen moons of the year.

TRADITIONAL CRAFTS AND ACTIVITIES

- Getting the garden ready for planting,

- sowing seeds.

- Egg dyeing and decorating.

- Filling vases with spring flowers and bringing the outdoors indoors.

- Spring-cleaning.

SYMBOLS

Hares, serpents, eggs, greenery, flowers, solar crosses, solar wheels, sun symbols.

MAGICAL HERBS

Acacia, almond, benzoin, birch, bistort, blackthorn, cleavers, coltsfoot, daisy, forget-me-not, frankincense, gorse, ground ivy, lemon verbena, nettle, pine, primrose, tansy, violet.

Personal Spring Equinox Ritual

You will need:

> GREEN CANDLE
>
> YELLOW CANDLE
>
> SPRING FLOWERS
>
> GREEN LEAVES

Invoke your sacred space.

Say,

> *I stand at a moment of balance*
> *But cross the threshold into the light half of the year*
> *When all renews.*

Light the green candle and say,

> *The goddess of spring walks among us*
> *Garlanding the earth with beauty.*
> *Come, maiden and our beloved one.*

Light the yellow candle and say,

> *The lord of the sun draws closer*
> *Warming the land beneath our feet.*
> *Come, golden lord and our beloved one.*

Lay the spring flowers before the green candle (or goddess image), saying,

> *I make this offering to the maiden of the earth in gratitude.*
> *Lady, bless the seeds.*
> *Bless the land with growth*
> *Bless the animals with fertility and give them your protection*
> *Lady, give me your blessings.*
> *Let all be blessed in your name, maiden and beloved one.*

Lay the green leaves before the yellow candle (or god image), saying,

> *I make this offering to the lord in gratitude.*
> *Lord, bless us with illumination*
> *Lord, bless us with warmth*
> *As we step into the light.*
> *Let all be blessed in your name, our lord and beloved one.*

Meditate on this for a while. When you are ready, say,

> *This is a time of transformation*
> *When all awakens and renews.*
> *Maiden of the earth*

Awaken the parts of me that need awakening
So that I may be as a seed that stirs
And blossoms into the light.
Bright lord of the sun
Awaken my inner fire
Light my path forward
And warm my heart with love.

Meditate on this and be open to inner guidance. When you are ready to close, say,

Lord and Lady, I thank you for your presence and your blessings this night. Let the candles be put out but let me remember the lessons of this night. The rite is over. Blessed be.

Close your sacred space.

Beltane

In Ireland, the first of May was called Bealtaine/Beltene, with the modern Irish spelling of *Beltane*, which means something like "bright fire." The extended hours of daylight are very noticeable, and in the solar calendar, it marks the real coming of summer. Nature bursts with potent energy, life, and growth, and all about us the earth flowers, and young animals are born. May Day was celebrated by bringing in the May (hawthorn blossom), collecting armfuls of flowers and greenery for decoration, maypole dancing, electing the May queen and king, and bonfires blazing across the hilltops.

With its powerful magic, Beltane is one of the three great spirit nights of the year (the others are Midsummer and Samhain) when the otherworld is close, and fairy connection is easier to make. They meet beneath the shade of the hawthorn tree, and according to English folklore, any human who sleeps beneath a hawthorn tree at Beltane is in danger of being taken away by the fay.

As the wheel of the year turns to summer, we celebrate the sacred marriage of the Lord and Lady. Their passion and fire ignite the fertility of the land. They come together in love, the most powerful force in the universe, which binds spirit and matter together, creating the world from opposites.

It is a time of beauty, love, and joy when we look to our own connections and rekindle our own passion for life.

THEMES OF BELTANE

- Sexual energy

- Passion

- Mating and pairing

- Love in all its forms

- Connection

- Celebration and joy

- Flowering and blossoming

- Nature's abundance

- Fertility

- Activity, expansion, growth

- The Green Man

- Summer goddess

- Closeness of the otherworld

- Fairy contact

- The spiritual manifested in the physical

- Energy

- Fire

- What ignites your fire and passion?

- How do you interweave the physical and spiritual?

TRADITIONAL FOODS

There are now fresh seasonal foods available from the garden (such as spring cabbage, rhubarb, herbs, broad beans, early lettuce, spring onions, radishes, and early new potatoes), Try adding edible flower petals to salads (primrose, hawthorn, violet, cowslip) or freshly foraged leaves, such as dandelion, dill, hawthorn, sorrel, and chickweed. Traditional cottage dishes at this time included sorrel soup, nettle pudding, and nettle soup. Drink hawthorn flower wine, cowslip wine, or flower teas made from edible flowers.

TRADITIONAL CRAFTS AND ACTIVITIES

- Maypole dancing

- May king and queen election

- Feasts and celebrations to welcome the summer

- Bonfires

- Jumping the fire for purification

- Gathering greenery and flowers

- Hawthorn blossom

- Making and wearing flower chaplets

- Making flower blossom wines (hawthorn, cowslip, dandelion, gorse, etc.)

- Making early summer flower tinctures and salves

- Perform love spells and fertility magic

- Placing wards on the home, stables, and outbuildings

SYMBOLS

Maypoles, phallic symbols, hobby horses, colourful ribbons, seasonal flowers and greenery, blossoming tree branches.

MAGICAL HERBS

Hawthorn flowers, apple blossom, primrose, violet, cowslip, dandelion, sorrel, chickweed, nettle, birch, celandine, cinquefoil, clover, cuckoo pint, daisy, honeysuckle, horse chestnut flowers, lily of the valley, sorrel, sweet cicely, woodruff.

Personal Beltane Rite
You will need:

> RED ROSE
>
> WHITE ROSE
>
> GODDESS STATUE
>
> GOD STATUE

GOLD RIBBON

CUP OF WHITE WINE WITH WHITE ROSE PETALS FLOATING ON TOP

ATHAME OR KNIFE

GOLD CANDLE

Invoke your sacred space.

Lay the white roses before the goddess image and the red roses before the god image.

Light the gold candle and say,

> Lord and Lady, witness that I come here tonight to seek the mystery of union.

Take up the white rose and say,

> White rose, you symbolise purity and innocence, you stand for the goddess who is the mother of us all. In your folded petals, you conceal a secret inner core; your heart is unknown, the hidden sacred world. To contemplate you is to contemplate the mystery of existence.

Meditate on this for a while.

Take up the red rose and say,

> Red rose, you symbolise earthly passion and fertility, you stand for the god, who is the father of us all. Your petals are rayed, like the ever-renewing strength of the sun. Your solar rays symbolise the journey of life, death, and rebirth. Yours is the path of immortality through death.

Meditate on this for a while.

Bind the two roses with the gold ribbon and say,

> The red and the white together signify the union of opposites, the mystical marriage of Lady and Lord, which reconciles male and female, summer and winter, life and death, flesh and spirit, and brings about all creation, driven by the most fundamental and powerful force in the universe: love.

Meditate on this for a while and say,

> As these opposites unite, so our souls yearn to be united with the divine. In this sacred marriage the individual ego must dissolve and become one with the whole in transcendent unity. We long to melt into the beauty of the divine, surrendering the old self for the higher soul within.

Plunge the athame into the cup. Meditate on what this signifies.

Drink the wine then say,

> *God and goddess, we are reborn through your mysteries. All else is silence. This rite is*
> *ended, blessed be.*

Close your sacred space. Allow the candle to burn itself out.

<p style="text-align:center">~~~~~~~~</p>

Midsummer—The Summer Solstice

The summer solstice is celebrated on the longest day, the time of greatest light; we call it Midsummer. Heat blazes across the land, and the cold dark days of winter seem far away. Now is the time of brightness, long days, and warmth. This is the season of greatest growth when foliage and flowering are at their fullest. On this, the second of the three great spirit nights, fairies are at their most active. And as the mist gate forms in the warm air rising, the entrance to the otherworld opens. On this night the future can be uncovered.

Father Sun is in his glory, beaming his radiant life-giving energy into the world. He is strong and virile, the husband and lover of Mother Earth. His fire kindles the goddess to swell with fruit so that autumn and harvest can come. His is a power greater than any individual life; he is eternal truth, justice, and enlightenment. Father Sun fills all things with a spiritual light and brings the realisation that life is not mundane drudgery, but spiritual and eternal. His light banishes all shadows, fears, and illusions. He is the light within your soul that connects you to the soul light in all other beings and enables you to see things from beyond your individual awareness.

At the Midsummer, you can connect with Father Sun at the peak of his power and absorb the energy of abundance, love, and higher consciousness. Take this opportunity to fuel your inner fire and fill yourself with vital life force.

THEMES OF MIDSUMMER

- The time of greatest light

- Father Sun at his time of glory

- The consummation of Father Sun and Mother Earth

- The fertilization of Mother Earth

- The seasonal triumph of vegetation

- Bonfires and jumping through them for luck and protection

- Inner illumination

- Fairy contact

- Divination

- Harvesting herbs

- Acknowledgment that after this, light declines

Traditional Foods

By this time of year, food is plentiful with salad vegetables, soft fruits, and herbs in peak condition. This is the best time for picking most herbs, and they obtain potent virtues for magic on the solstice and should be included in the feast. Traditional foods include watercress soup, herb tarts, elderflower fritters, gooseberry fool, and soft fruit tarts.

Traditional Crafts and Activities

- Outdoor celebrations with group/family/friends

- Circle dancing

- Merrymaking, feasting

- Bonfires

- Torchlight processions

- Witnessing the rising and setting of the of sun

- Bathing in healing waters

- Divination

- Love magic

- Handfastings

- Gather herbs and flowers

Symbols

Sun wheels, sun, fire, bonfires, roses, rosettes, daisies, all rayed flowers, herbs, equal-armed crosses, torches.

Magical Herbs

Alexanders, angelica, ash, bay, calendula, camomile, celandine, daisy, dill, dog rose, elder, elecampane, fennel, fern, feverfew, fir, frankincense, heather, honeysuckle, lavender, marjoram, mint, mistletoe, oak, rose, St. John's wort, strawberry, sunflower, sweet cicely, vervain, violet, yarrow.

Personal Midsummer Ritual

This ritual should be performed at dawn on the summer solstice, the longest day. Do it outdoors if you can. You will need:

WINE FOR OFFERING

BONFIRE (IF YOU WISH)

Call sacred space. Light your fire if you are having one. When you see the sun rising above the horizon, say,

> O lord of greatest light
> The birds sing at your rising.
> Now is the time of your glory and power.
> Your long embrace of Mother Earth.
> Is the giver of life.
> Your arrows of light protect us
> From all the powers of darkness.
> Father Sun, far traveller who sees all
> You are the eye of the sky, you behold everything.
> Behold me here as I honour you.

Watch and wait as the sun rises. Observe how its light spreads across the land and how its energy awakens the birds and animals. When the full sun is visible, say,

> Father Sun, I stand in your light
> The pulsing life force that invigorates all things.
> I breathe it in and let it fill me
> Illuminating every cell of my body.
> All cares and ills dissolve like the morning mist
> In the sun's radiance.
> Father Sun, I fill myself with your power
> And am divinely alive.

Absorb the power of the sun's light into your body through your breath, through your skin. Feel it spread and warm every cell of your body, purifying and energising. Spend as long as you need. When you are ready, say,

> *Father Sun, in this time of splendour*
> *Light the path of my soul's calling.*
> *May I embrace the light within me*
> *And know the radiance of my spirit.*
> *Let your illumination grow within me.*

Reflect on this for a few moments. Pick up the wine and say,

> *Father Sun and Mother Earth*
> *Ancient and abundant ones*
> *I make you this offering.*

Pour the wine on the earth, saying,

> *Father Sun and Mother Earth*
> *Grant us fair woodlands and green fields*
> *Grant us orchards of fullness and corn risen high.*
> *Grant us herbs of healing and roots of power.*
> *We rejoice in your blessings.*

Hold your hands to the earth and say,

> *I give honour to the joining of Father Sun and Mother Earth.*

Spend as long as you wish in contemplation. If you wish, you can now perform divinations as the day is especially propitious for this. When you are ready to close, say,

> *I have celebrated the rite of Midsummer. I have acknowledged the blessings of Father Sun and Mother Earth and have done them honour. The rite is ended in peace and love. Blessed be.*

Close your sacred space.

Lughnasa/Lammas

Lughnasa takes its name from Gaelic and means the *násad* (games or an assembly) of Lugh, a Celtic deity, as it was a time when the Irish held tribal assemblies.

It is celebrated as a harvest festival, marking the end of the period of summer growth and the beginning of the harvest; the Irish accounted it the first day of autumn. Lughnasa marks the fruition of the agricultural year's work with the weaning of calves and lambs, the ripening of the grain and the first apples, pears, bilberries, blackberries, and grapes.

We celebrate it as the time that Mother Earth gives birth to the fruits of the land, the beginning of the harvest. We honour the bounty of the earth and in gratitude, we offer the first fruits (the first of the harvest) to the Gods. Expressing gratitude is an important spiritual practice. We can thank the Gods for the things we have (as opposed to the things we think we want), like a home, clean water, enough food, and the beauty and abundance of the planet we live on. It makes us think about the good things in our lives, instead of concentrating on the bad, and connects us to something bigger than ourselves.

THEMES OF LUGHNASA

- The end of summer and the start of autumn

- The end of the hungry time and the return of plenty

- Mother Earth gives birth to the harvest

- The start of the harvest

- The offering of first fruits to the Gods

- Gratitude

- The vegetation god embodied within the first fruits

- Eating the god/communing with the god in bread and wine

- Honouring and thanking the Gods

- Feasting

Traditional Foods

This is the time of summer ripeness, with an abundance of fresh produce including tomatoes, cucumbers, onions, baby carrots, broccoli, cabbage, beetroot, cauliflowers, fresh salad, courgettes, beans, and peppers. Lughnasa is also the start of the apple and grape harvest, and there are ripe fruits such as peaches, apricots, gooseberries, and plums. The special ritual foods of Lughnasa are apple, basil, borage, chicory, fenugreek, fennel, honeysuckle, poppy seeds, grapes, vine leaves, and nasturtium flowers, as well as new potatoes, bilberries and other soft fruit, apples, wine, beer, and bread. An old custom was to pick the first apples and make them into a drink called Lammas wool. Make melomels (fruit mead) and fruit wines, such as peach, apple, gooseberry, and so on.

Traditional Crafts and Activities

- Assemblies on hilltops

- Pilgrimages

- Drinking and feasting

- Dancing

- Games and competitions

- Placing flowers at water sources

- Baking bread

- Making donations to the less fortunate

Symbols

Bread, wine, sheaves of grain, ears of corn, grapes, fruits

Magical Herbs

Alder, apple, basil, benzoin, borage, chicory, daisy, fennel, fenugreek, frankincense, gorse, honeysuckle, ivy, marshmallow, mugwort, nasturtium, oak, pine, poppy, sunflower, vine, woad

Personal Rite for Lughnasa

Decorate the ritual area with fruits and grain. You will also need:

BREAD

WINE OR FRUIT JUICE

ONE GREEN CANDLE

ONE GOLD CANDLE

ONE WHITE CANDLE

OFFERING DISH

Open your sacred space and say,

> *I come to celebrate the rite of Lughnasa at the start of the harvest. Under the golden light of Father Sun, Mother Earth gives birth to the grain and fruit. I come to offer thanks for their gifts.*

Light the green candle and say,

> *I call to you, Mother Earth*
> *Mother Earth, your body supports me.*
> *Mother Earth, your nurturing power sustains me.*
> *Mother Earth, your fields and orchards feed me.*

Light the gold candle and say,

> *I call to you Father Sun*
> *Father Sun, your light fills my spirit.*
> *Father Sun, your energy gives me life.*
> *Father Sun, you illuminate my spirit.*

Light the white candle and say,

> *Mother Earth, Father Sun*
> *You hold me in the great web of life*
> *Where we are all one.*

Pour some of the wine into the offering bowl and say,

> *The first of the harvest is always for the Gods.*
> *I drink, yet it is not wine I drink, but the love of the goddess flowing through the growing vines and trees, fruit ripening under the sun. I drink and salute Mother Earth, praying that she will guard the fruit until the harvest is complete. May it be good!*

Drink some of the wine. Put some of the bread into the offering bowl, saying,

> *The first of the harvest is always for the Gods.*
> *I eat, but it is not bread I eat, but the power of the sun, sprung from the womb of the earth. I eat and salute Father Sun, praying that he will guard the grain until the harvest is complete. May the crops be good!*

Eat some of the bread.

Spend some time thinking about what you are grateful for (you can add to the following list). When you are ready, say,

> *I give gratitude for the beautiful earth.*
> *I give gratitude for the light of the sun.*
> *I give gratitude for the seeds, the buds, and the harvest.*
> *I give gratitude for the food I eat and the air I breathe.*
> *I give gratitude for the wide oceans and the mountain streams.*
> *I give gratitude for the stag and the hare, the salmon and the hawk.*
> *I give gratitude for the crawling beings and the swimming beings.*
> *I give gratitude for my hearth and home and the fire within.*
> *I give gratitude for my kith and kin.*
> *I give gratitude for the great web of life*
> *Where we are all one.*

Take a piece of bread and place it in the north of your sacred space, saying,

> *May there be peace in the north.*

Take a piece of bread and place it in the east of your sacred space, saying,

> *May there be peace in the east.*

Take a piece of bread and place it in the south of your sacred space, saying,

> *May there be peace in the south.*

Take a piece of bread and place it in the west of your sacred space, saying,

> *May there be peace in the west.*

Reflect on this. When you are ready to finish, say,

Father Sun and Mother Earth, I have honoured you and given thanks for your gifts.
Grant me your blessings. This rite is ended. Blessed be.

Put out the candles. Close your sacred space.

Herfest—The Autumn Equinox

At the autumn equinox, day and night stand equal once more, but the dark is gaining. Afterward the hours of darkness progressively become greater than the hours of light, with dawn getting later and sunset getting earlier each day—a process that will continue until the winter solstice. Father Sun is weakening, and the weather is getting colder. The year is in decline.

The autumn equinox, which we call Herfest, is the harvest festival that marks the culmination of all the work of the agricultural year. We celebrate harvest home with festivities and feasts and make the corn dolly from the last of the grain to be cut. We collect ripe red apples, sticky blackberries, and elderberries in the hedgerows. We go picking and nutting and spend our time preserving and storing, cider making and beer brewing, readying ourselves for the winter to come. We give thanks to the Gods for all they have given us during the year.

At the autumn equinox, the expansive part of the year is over, and it is time to turn inward. We celebrate one of the deepest mysteries and remember that this is also a festival of sacrifice, as the bright god of vegetation is cut down so that we may eat. He departs from us to go into the underworld (the seed is returned to the earth in the autumn). Through that death comes transformation, regeneration, and rebirth. The lesson of nature is that it is only through this process that spiritual illumination comes.

Father Sun's power is decreasing, but deprived of the external light, we may encounter inner illumination. This is an opportunity to turn your attention from material concerns and focus your attention inward, a time when you can experience profound insights. This is the season of *sacrifice*, a word that means "to make sacred." Sometimes you have to surrender cherished beliefs, dreams, habits, deep-seated anger, desires, or bad relationships that no longer serve you to reconnect with your life's purpose.

THEMES OF THE AUTUMN EQUINOX

- Harvest, abundance

- Bread, wine, corn, feasting

- Giving thanks to the Gods for their gifts

- Sacrifice of the grain god so that we may eat

- The god goes into the underworld

- The mystery of death and transformation

- The mystery of the seed in the earth

- Balance of light and dark

- Entering the dark half of the year

- What gifts have you received this year?

- What have you harvested this year?

- What do you need to sacrifice to progress?

- The eternal return

Traditional Foods

This is the time of plenty with a profusion of foods available, including main crop potatoes; mature root vegetables such as carrots, swedes, turnips, and beetroot; cauliflower and broccoli; beans; and the last of the fresh salads, tomatoes, wild nuts, and mushrooms. It is a busy time when the harvest must be gathered before the first frosts, and food must be prepared, stored, and preserved for the dead time of winter. The special ritual foods of the occasion include apples, acorns, basil, beans, blackberries, corn, chicory, rose hips, parsley, poppy seeds, hazel and other nuts, and hawthorn berries. Traditionally the harvest loaf is plaited or shaped into wheat sheaf shapes.

Traditional Crafts and Activities

- Harvest feasts

- Breadmaking

- Making corn dollies

- Harvesting garden produce

- Apple gathering

- Foraging for fruits, nuts, and fungi

- Making jams, preserves, and wine

Symbols

Corn dollies, fruits, grains, bread, wine

Magical Herbs

Acorn, alder, apple, ash, basil, bean, benzoin, blackberry, buckwheat, calendula, cedar, chicory, grains, cornflower, cypress, daisy, dog rose, elder, frankincense, hazel, ivy, myrrh, parsley, poppy.

Personal Autumn Equinox Ritual

The altar is decorated with autumn fruits, leaves, and grain. Make a corn dolly, which is placed on the altar. You will need:

>AUTUMN FRUITS, LEAVES, AND GRAIN
>
>SHEAF OF GRAIN
>
>CORN DOLLY
>
>GOLD CANDLE
>
>BROWN CANDLE
>
>WHITE CANDLE
>
>BREAD
>
>WINE (OR FRUIT JUICE)

Open your sacred space. When you are ready, say,

>*Day and night stand equal*
>*But the wheel turns*
>*And the year falls into darkness.*

Light the brown candle and say,

>I *honour you, Mother Earth*
>*You have brought forth the fruit and grain.*
>*The seeds shall be returned to the sleeping ground*
>*Waiting for rebirth as the wheel turns.*

Light the gold candle and say,

>I *honour you, Father Sun*
>*You have given us light and warmth*
>*But now you sink to the west*

Waiting for rebirth as the wheel turns.

Mother Earth, Father Sun, your eternal dance of love gives life and death in its season.

Take up the sheaf of grain and say,

You have grown in the warmth of the summer sun. You grant us nourishment in the time that is to come. I give thanks.

I give thanks to the Lord and Lady for my own harvest this year, the things that I have achieved, actions grown from the seeds of my thoughts.

Reflect on these. Lay down the grain. Say:

The wheel turns.
The time of cold and dark comes
And we face the greatest mystery.
As the god travels into the darkness
We remember that he shall come again.
Now we too turn inward, following
The twisting labyrinth of the soul's journey
In the footsteps of the god
As he shall be reborn with the light
We too shall come to rebirth.

Lighting the white candle, say,

The goddess hears, the goddess answers, and the god will return.

Reflect on this. If you wish, you can celebrate with bread and wine. When you are ready to close, say,

I give thanks to the Lord and Lady for all that I have received throughout the year. I have harvested their gifts and set them aside, ready, for the time of darkness is upon us. I know that though the god goes into darkness, he shall come again. This rite is ended, blessed be.

Close your sacred space.

Samhain

Samhain is the start of winter. The hours of daylight continue to dwindle; the powers of growth are winding down, while the powers of darkness and cold gain ascendancy. Plant growth has stopped. The vegetation harvest has long been gathered in, and root crops, nuts, berries, and apples have been stored against hungry winter. Animals have been brought down from their summer pastures to more sheltered winter quarters to be fed on stored hay. We turn to the hearth and the warmth of the crackling fire and the cheer of the singing kettle on the hob.

We enter the season of the crone, the hag of winter. She is no gentle old lady, but wild, fierce, and primal, just like winter itself. With her holly staff in her hand and a carrion crow perched on her shoulder, she strides across the land, beating down the vegetation and hardening the earth with ice. But when the earth is bare and the trees are skeletal, when everything showy is stripped away, we feel the underlying bones of creation and we see more clearly into its deepest secrets; we approach its elemental power.

The myths of the crone tell us something fundamental about winter; there is a deep connection between fertility and winter death. While the maiden begins it, the mother bears it, and the harvest queen reaps it, the fertility of the next year's harvest is fundamentally the crone's gift—the sleeping seeds in the underworld are in her care.

Winter is a powerful time of radical change. We should not mourn the passing of spring and summer, but celebrate life returned to the cauldron of creation where it is held, where the compost of the old feeds the roots and seeds of the new.

Though the modern world insists that we should be the same all year round, our bodies tell us that this is not so. Winter affects us on a physical, emotional, and spiritual level, and we need to acknowledge that we too are cyclical beings. Mother Earth teaches us that periods of withdrawal from busyness, slowing down, resting, and recuperating are necessary.

All growth takes place in darkness from idea in the mind to seed in the ground. We withdraw our energies into our roots and nurture the seeds sleeping in the darkness. We undertake deep inner work and dreaming magic. Samhain is a chance to enter the crone's cauldron of transformation, to shed our old forms and use them as fuel for new ones.

Samhain is time to acknowledge the role of death, seasonally and personally. We all return to Mother Earth, and death is the price we pay for life. Our lives are ephemeral, existing in a time that passes. Time will destroy all, and all things dissolve in the blackness of the crone's cauldron. But the goddess promises us that the tomb is the womb from which we shall be reborn.

Death is an absolute transition from one state to another with no possibility of return. We experience many small deaths in our lives as various stages and experiences end to make way for new phases and experiences, up until the ultimate transformation of physical death and rebirth. Death initiates change. We take this time to acknowledge death in all its forms and to mourn what we need to mourn. We think of all the lives that have touched ours and the ancestors that have brought us to this place.

Themes of Samhain

- Summer's end

- Beginning of winter

- Entering the darkest part of the year

- Closing the season of agricultural work

- Death, culling, ending

- The tomb/mound is raised over the seed

- The goddess becomes the crone

- The cauldron of transformation

- The time of chaos begins (and goes on until Yule)

- The otherworld is close

- Feast of the dead

- Communion with the ancestors and the departed

- The god in the underworld (where he remains until Yule)

- What is ending in you?

- What do you need to let go of?

- What do you need to mourn?

TRADITIONAL FOODS

By Samhain we have usually had the first winter frosts where I live, and tender plants have been damaged or killed. The fresh salad season is over, but root vegetables are still viable in the ground. Ritual foods for Samhain include apples, parsley, sloes, pumpkin, hops, juniper and rowan, oats, grains, St. Catherine's cake, and Thor cake. Soul cakes are left out for the dead.

TRADITIONAL CRAFTS AND ACTIVITIES

- Divination

- Guising (fancy dress, from *dis-guising*) to hide your identity from the roaming spirits

- Bonfires to encourage the declining sun

- Placing candles in western windows to light the way for the dead

- Creating an ancestor altar with candles and photographs of deceased relatives and friends

- Holding a dumb feast where the spirits are invited to the table

- Telling ghost stories

SYMBOLS

Symbols of death, such as skulls. Closely associated with Halloween is the hollowed pumpkin or turnip, carved with a frightening face and lit with a candle inside. It is intended to frighten away the spirits that roam the land at this dangerous time.

MAGICAL HERBS

Aconite, alder, apple, aspen, belladonna, blackthorn, calamus, catnip, chervil, cypress, damiana, dittany of Crete, ivy, elder, fumitory, galangal, hellebore, hemlock, henbane, honeysuckle, hop, juniper, mullein, myrrh, parsley, pumpkin, rowan, thistle, valerian, wormwood, yew.

Personal Samhain Ritual
You will need:

> 1 WHITE ALTAR CANDLE
>
> 1 BLACK SPIRIT CANDLE
>
> PUMPKIN LANTERNS AND SKULLS, IF YOU WISH

PHOTOGRAPHS OF THE DEAD YOU WISH TO REMEMBER

JEWELLERY OR ITEMS BELONGING TO DEPARTED LOVED ONES

BARE TWIGS AND WITHERED LEAVES TO DECORATE THE ALTAR

Invoke your sacred space.

Invoke the goddess, saying,

> *Mother of all that lives, harvester of all that dies*
>
> *Crone of winter, I call upon you.*
>
> *This is the festival of Samhain*
>
> *When barren winter approaches*
>
> *When death stalks the land*
>
> *When many are called back to your womb*
>
> *To await another birth.*
>
> *Be with me tonight, dark crone, death crone*
>
> *And give me sight of these.*

Light a black spirit candle to call departed friends, family, and ancestors to your circle and say,

> *Harken now, you souls who wander*
>
> *Friends in life and friends in death*
>
> *Heed my call and come to this light.*
>
> *Ancestors; bone of my bone, seed of my seed*
>
> *I am here because you walked before me*
>
> *I am here because of your wisdom and courage*
>
> *I honour your memory on this Samhain Eve*
>
> *Ancestors, bone of my bone, seed of my seed*
>
> *Come to me and share this night.*

Spend some time in silent meditation, communing with the spirits who come to you or remembering those who have passed into the summerlands. Mourn what you need to mourn. When you have finished, say, in a firm voice,

> *Blessings be upon you, spirits of the summerlands.*
>
> *Let each of those spirits go now upon their way, harming not this world*
>
> *Travelling along the soul road toward rebirth*

> Knowing that we shall meet again some other Samhain night.
> I honour you and bid you farewell.

Put out the black spirit candle. When you are ready, say,

> Dark crone, keeper of the cauldron
> The crucible of death and rebirth.
> I trust in the mystery of the wheel of life.
> Every beginning has an ending
> And every ending is a new beginning.
> We live in a time that passes.
> Time will destroy all: prince and pauper
> Priest and warrior, city and state.
> In the grave, all worldly ambitions come to naught.
> All things dissolve in your cauldron;
> All things return to the source.
> But as the mound is raised above the seed
> The seed prepares itself for rebirth
> And all things are transformed by death.
> For this is the secret that only the wise may know:
> The tomb is the womb from which we shall be reborn.
> And I shall know rebirth and the light of another dawn.

Meditate on the profound mystery of death, consider what you need to let go of—what you need to surrender to the cauldron so that new things may come.

When you are ready to finish, say,

> Crone goddess, yours are the deepest mysteries.
> I thank you for your presence here tonight.
> It is not for me to dismiss you, instead
> I ask that you watch over me and guide me
> Guard me and protect me
> In the dark times.

Put out the altar candle. Close your sacred space. Say,

> This rite is ended, blessed be.

Yule—The Winter Solstice

We depend on Father Sun for life; in the summer, the long hours of daylight and warmth make the crops grow. In the winter days of darkness and cold, plants shrivel and die; humans and animals struggle to find food and survive. Each day, up to the winter solstice, the sun grows weaker and weaker. If it does not regenerate, then life must end. The word *solstice* comes from Latin and means "sun stands still." The sun usually rises at a different point on the horizon each day, but at the solstice, it seems to rest for three days in the same place, as though the wheel of time itself has been stilled.

But the wheel, briefly stilled, turns again. Then, in the very moment of greatest gloom, the sun is reborn. Life and hope are rekindled: the light will grow; warmth will increase; spring, summer, and the harvest will come. The old year, the old cycle of existence and time, dissolves back into the primordial chaos. The sun reborn and the new year represent the whole world rejuvenated, the wheel of the year restarted, and reality renewed.

The season of the crone of winter brings gloom and death, but just when bane and darkness threaten to overwhelm the world, there comes a pause, a breath before the cycle continues: the winter solstice. Hope is renewed in the time of greatest darkness. And this is a great mystery: it is the crone who restores order from chaos and brings life from death. She is the gatekeeper of transformation. She draws forth the mysterious hidden forces of life from the underworld and brings them to rebirth in the child of promise, the reborn sun.

THEMES OF YULE

- Rebirth of light, hope, renewal, regeneration

- The child of promise

- Light and hope in the time of greatest darkness

- Encouraging the sun with fire, light

- Evergreen life persisting in the time of death

- Order rescued from chaos

- Death of the old, birth of the new

- A time apart, a pause, a breath before the cycle continues

- Cessation of hostilities, peace and goodwill

- The levelling of social barriers, a reversal of social order

- Reward and punishment for the deeds of the year; a time of reckoning

- What ending do you seek, and what do you need to leave behind?

- What rebirth do you seek?

TRADITIONAL FOODS

In the past, little fresh food was available at this time, but Yule was a time of great feasting and merrymaking when special, carefully hoarded and stored foods, such as sweets, costly spices, liqueurs, and spirits, were brought out to celebrate the rebirth of the sun and impart a little cheer in the depths of winter. Chestnuts, dried fruit, oranges (representing fire and the sun), wassail, mulled wine, eggnog, fruitcake, mince pies, and plum pudding.

TRADITIONAL CRAFTS AND ACTIVITIES

- Bringing in the green from the hedgerows: holly, ivy, mistletoe, rosemary, and bay

- Decorating with evergreens

- Wassailing

- Gift making

- Gift giving

- Feasting as a pledge of faith that the year will be renewed and the next harvest will come

SYMBOLS

Evergreen foliage—holly, ivy, mistletoe, rosemary, bay. Sacred trees honoured and brought indoors. Lights against the darkness. Spherical (sun-shaped) decorations on the tree.

MAGICAL HERBS

Apple, bayberry, blackthorn, bay, calendula, cinnamon, cypress, frankincense, holly, ivy, juniper, mistletoe, oak, orange, pine, rosemary.

Personal Rite for Yule

You will need:

CAULDRON OR LARGE POT

GOLD CANDLE IN THE CAULDRON

ALTAR CANDLES OF RED AND GREEN

TEALIGHTS

Open your sacred space. Light the altar candles. Say,

In the coldness of winter, we hunger.
In the stillness of winter, we are silent.
We need the fire in our hearts to love.
We need the fire in the hearth to eat.
We need the fire in the head to make.
We need the fire in the heavens to live.

Invoke the goddess with these words:

Lady of night, lady of barren woodlands
Lady of the crystal snows, I call upon you.
Mistress of life, mistress of death
You who guards the gateway to mysteries of rebirth
I call to you. Be with me in this circle.

Pause for a while, then say,

The year has reached its lowest ebb
All is darkness and death.
Yet in this darkness we must find hope.
In this darkness we must find light.
The wheel of the year, which has been stilled
Must spin on.
The sun must be reborn!

Pause for a while to meditate on this, then say,

On the threshold of dawn, the sun king waits
The light of the world, gold light in black sky.

> On the rim of the world, the sun king dances
> Our child of promise, the sun king dances
> At his moment of birth, the sun king dances
> The light of our hope
> Gold light in black sky.
> On the threshold of dawn, the sun king waits.

Light the gold candle in the cauldron (if you are indoors, you can also put on the lights on the Yule tree) and say,

> The light is reborn!

Light a tealight from the gold candle in the cauldron to symbolise your hopes for the coming year and place it in the part of the circle most suitable—west for emotional matters and love; north for practical matters, health, and work; east for mental efforts and study; south for energy and creativity. Then say,

> With the sun we are each reborn. Life is renewed. Blessed be!

Meditation or acts of magic may be performed. Bread and wine may follow, if you wish. When you are ready to close, say,

> I have celebrated the rite of Yule. I have honoured the crone and the reborn sun. I give
> them my blessing and my thanks. I shall go forth with hope in my heart, safe in the
> knowledge that the wheel shall turn. Blessed be.

Close your sacred space. Let the cauldron candle burn itself out.

CHAPTER 15

. . . .

Cycles of the Moon

When the moon rises, she sheds her silvery light on the land. How different everything looks and feels from the daylight. While Father Sun rules the day, Lady Moon rules the night. Hers is a hidden realm of shifting shadows, of nightmares and dreams, of magic and secrets.

She is the lady of changes who constantly transforms herself. Beginning in darkness, she first emerges as a maiden with her thin crescent bow, then grows to the moon's first quarter seven days later. In another week, she reaches her pregnant fullness, a shining silver disc in the sky. For three days, she is the mother moon with maximum brilliance. Then, she begins to age and shrink, waning to a half-moon in seven days, then diminishing to the crone with her sickle. Finally, she is swallowed by darkness for three days. But within the darkness, all potentials are contained, and just as all life generates in the dark of the womb, the dark mother renews herself, begins life anew, and returns to us as maiden when the crescent moon emerges once more.

The goddess of the moon has had many names: Artemis, Selene, Diana, Luna, Devana, and so on. Just like the phases of the moon, some moon goddesses are virginal and chaste, some are fertile mothers, and some are aged crones, reflecting the whole cycle of a woman's life. Women often refer to their days of menstruation as their moon time, the womb waxing and waning over the course of a month, just as the moon does.

. . . . .

No wonder the old witches met under the full moon to cast their spells and collected certain herbs by moonlight. Lady Moon speaks to us about the hidden power behind creation, the vast ocean of potential holding all within it: past, present, and future. The magic of the moon is subtle, but gently potent, opening the way to dreams, to increased psychic abilities, to inspiration and spiritual insight, to the alchemy of change and personal transformation.

Phases of the Moon

WAXING MOON

WAXING CRESCENT: 1 to 49 percent of the moon is lit on the right side (in the southern hemisphere it is the left side).

FIRST QUARTER: 50 percent of the moon is lit seven days after the emergence of the new moon.

WAXING GIBBOUS: The moon is lit 51 to 99 percent.

FULL MOON: When the disc of the moon is completely illuminated for three days.

WANING MOON

WANING GIBBOUS: The left side of the moon is lit 99 to 51 percent on the left side (southern hemisphere right side).

LAST QUARTER: Lit 50 percent seven days after the full moon.

WANING CRESCENT: Lit 49 to 1 percent.

DARK MOON: When the whole disc of the moon is in the earth's shadow for three days.

Waxing Moon Magic

Under the auspices of the maiden moon goddess, waxing moon energy concerns growth, increase, and surging power. It is a time for magic of new beginnings, things that will grow to fullness in the future—starting new projects, new relationships, planting, making plans, laying a foundation, making positive changes, healing emotional issues. Anything you do to strengthen your body, to fortify yourself, is much more effective when the moon is waxing.

DRAWING DOWN THE MOON RITUAL

Most witches will have heard the phrase "drawing down the moon." In Gardnerian and Alexandrian witchcraft, it relates to the high priest drawing down power into the high priestess, but it has much older antecedents of drawing down the power of the waxing moon (not the full moon) itself into a glass or silver vessel of liquid, which is drunk to imbibe the power of the waxing moon for healing and blessing.

You will need the following:

BOWL OF GLASS OR SILVER

SMALL ROUND MIRROR

SPRING WATER OR WHITE WINE

Go out on one of the first evenings of the waxing moon just after sunset to somewhere you can see the moon clearly.

Pour the water into the bowl. Angle the mirror so that the moon is reflected into the bowl from the mirror. Notice that the waxing moon, bringer of growth, is reflected in the bowl as the waning moon, bringer of wisdom. Call on Lady Moon to instil her magical power into your bowl, saying,

> *Maiden of the waxing moon*
> *Draw your silver bow*
> *And shoot down arrows of moonbeams*
> *To charge this potion.*
> *Maiden of the moon, I call to you.*

Wait until you feel the liquid is charged. Pour a few drops onto the earth so that moon magic may flow to the earth. Say,

> *Drinking from this vessel*
> *I drink the essence of Lady Moon*
> *I kiss my hand to the waxing moon*
> *I pray to the lady that she will make me whole*
> *And grant me blessings.*

Drink the wine/water in communion. Feel the power of the waxing moon flow into you. When you have finished, say,

> *Maiden of the waxing moon, I honour you and give you thanks for your blessings. Blessed be.*

PROTECTION WAXING MOON RITUAL

This ritual calls upon Artemis, waxing moon goddess, wild huntress, protector and defender of women, but you may prefer to call upon a waxing moon goddess from your own tradition. Perform after the moon has risen; if you can do it outside in full view of the moon, this will be more powerful. You will need the following:

SMALL TABLE TO USE AS YOUR ALTAR

NIGHT-BLOOMING OR WHITE FLOWERS

GLASS BOWL OF SPRING WATER

2 SILVER CANDLES IN SILVER HOLDERS

1 WHITE TEALIGHT ON A SILVER DISH

WAXING MOON INCENSE (PAGE 75)

MOONCAKES ON A SILVER DISH (PAGE 160)

MATCHES

A PICTURE OR STATUE OF A WAXING MOON GODDESS

Wear white or silver clothes/robes and silver jewellery. Decorate the altar with night-blooming white flowers such as nicotiana, jasmine, moonflower, or tuberose. If you don't have these, use moon-associated white flowers such as white roses or lilies. Have a glass bowl filled with spring water on the altar. Place a statue or picture of Artemis (or your chosen waxing moon goddess) on the altar, with a white tealight on a silver dish in front of it. Have ready a dish of mooncakes (see below) on a white or silver plate.

Light the incense and the two silver candles. Say,

> *Artemis*
> *Pale lady of the midnight sky*
> *Hunting with your silver bow*
> *And moonbeam arrows.*
> *You, who wander the wild places*
> *You, who are wild and free*
> *Artemis, I call to you.*

Light the tealight. Say,

> Artemis
> You are the protector of women
> Swift in their defence
> You hear all who call for your aid
> Hear me now.
> I offer you this bowl of spring water
> Shining with reflected light.
> I offer you incense
> I offer you sweet-scented flowers
> I offer you mooncakes, baked with love.

Place one of the mooncakes before the image of the goddess. Say,

> Artemis
> Hear me now
> I call for your aid
> Protect me, goddess
> Grant me courage and independence
> That I may follow you in the woods and wild places
> Strong and free, as you are.
> Artemis, inspire me.

Spend some time thinking about this. Eat one of the cakes.

You may perform some other waxing moon magic if you wish, but communion with the goddess is the primary purpose of this ritual. When you have finished, say,

> Pale lady of the midnight sky
> You, who wander the wild places
> You, who are wild and free
> I give you my thanks and blessings.
> This rite is ended. Blessed be.

Allow the candles to burn out.

. . . .

Mooncakes

Gather the following ingredients.

- 200 GRAMS (1½ CUPS + 2 TABLESPOONS) PLAIN WHITE FLOUR (ALL-PURPOSE FLOUR)
- 4 TEASPOONS BAKING POWDER
- 1 TABLESPOON SUGAR
- 50 GRAMS (3 TABLESPOONS + 2 TEASPOONS) BUTTER
- 140 MILLILITRES (½ CUP) MILK

Sift the flour and baking powder into a bowl. Add the sugar. Chop the butter and blend with your fingertips into the flour until the mixture resembles fine breadcrumbs. Add the milk. The dough will be fairly sticky. Turn out onto a floured board. Roll out to an inch (3 centimetres) thick.

Using a round pastry cutter, cut the dough into crescent shapes. Brush the tops with milk and lay on a baking tray. Bake at 220 degrees Celsius, fan 200 degrees Celsius, 425 degrees Fahrenheit, gas 7 for fifteen minutes or until lightly browned. Cool on a wire rack.

Love Drawing Moon Spell

Mix white and red rose petals, lavender flowers, and white clover flowers when the moon is waxing. Divide them into three parts. Take one part outside and scatter it before the moon. Go into your bedroom. Sprinkle one part on the floor. Wrap the remaining part in a red cloth, tie with red cord, and say,

> *Silver lady of the night*
> *Who draws the crescent bow*
> *Softly, silently, silver moon*
> *Draw my love to me.*

Carry this on your person.

Waxing Moon Gardening

The waxing moon is a time for new beginnings, things that will grow to fullness in the future. As the earth breathes out, sap rises and growth above soil is favoured. A waxing moon is the best time to sow and plant anything that yields a harvest above the soil, including flowers and blooms. In the first week following the new moon, sow leafy vegetables and plants whose flowers and seeds are the edible part. Lawns also grow well when planted at the waxing moon. Do not prune during the waxing moon, as the sap is rising in plants, and they will "bleed" heavily. Repot plants during the waxing moon, as they will recover and grow better than if done at the waning moon.

Full Moon Magic

The goddess of the full moon is the pregnant mother. The energy of the full moon is fertile and beneficial. Full moon magic concerns the creative forces in the world and is used for positive magic—healing, blessing, love, friendship, success, and charging potions under the moon. Psychic abilities and magical skills are also enhanced under the full moon, so take the opportunity for scrying and other psychic work. Consecrate your magical tools under the full moon to boost their power.

The full moon is celebrated by witches as an esbat. Rituals celebrated at the esbats are determined by the energy of the time of year.

JANUARY, WOLF MOON: rites of hearth and home

FEBRUARY, STAY HOME MOON: rites of renewal, healing, and consecration

MARCH, WIND MOON: rites of seed sowing and blessing

APRIL, CUCKOO MOON: rites of love, beauty, and self-blessing

MAY, HARE MOON: rites of fertility in all its forms

JUNE, MEAD MOON: rites of fertility and handfastings

JULY, HAY MOON: rites of abundance and success

AUGUST, FRUIT MOON: rites of gratitude for what has been received

SEPTEMBER, HARVEST MOON: rites of thanksgiving, justice, and balance

OCTOBER, BLOOD MOON: divination and scrying

NOVEMBER, FOG MOON: rituals of protection and warding

DECEMBER, DARKEST DEPTHS MOON: rites of rebirth and renewal

SELF-BLESSING ESBAT RITUAL

For this ceremony, you will need the following:

STATUE OR IMAGE OF A FULL MOON GODDESS

SILVER CANDLE

WHITE FLOWERS OR NIGHT-BLOOMING FLOWERS

SELF-BLESSING OIL (PAGE 80)

FULL MOON INCENSE (PAGE 76)

Open your sacred space. Light the candle and say,

Lady Moon upon your throne
Silver queen of the night
Full bellied in the midnight sky.
You guard the sleep of children
And light the path of lovers.
You are my goddess and my guide.
I call upon you, lady, to be with me this night
To witness my desire.

Light the incense and say,

This is the time of fullness when all about opens, when I open myself to the joy of the world. I call upon you, silver queen and goddess, to witness my acts tonight and bless me, that I may walk in your ways.

Take the oil and anoint your feet. Say,

Blessed be my feet that shall walk your sacred paths.

Anoint your knees. Say,

Blessed be my knees that shall kneel before your sacred altars.

Anoint your breast. Say,

Blessed be my heart that shall be filled with love for you, and for all things.

Anoint your mouth. Say,

Blessed be my lips that shall speak your sacred words.

Anoint your forehead. Say,

> *Blessed be my self. Let me walk in love and blessing. Fill my heart with rejoicing, with beauty and strength, power and compassion, humour and humility, reverence and mirth. Silver goddess, bless your servant.*

Give thanks and close. Let the candle burn out.

FULL MOON SCRYING

Fill your cauldron or a black dish with water. Take it outside and place it so the full moon can be seen reflected in the water of the cauldron. Say,

> *Goddess of the moon*
> *Keeper of secrets*
> *Keeper of dreams*
> *Lift aside your veil*
> *And light my endeavours.*

There are no easy instructions for scrying; it is something that comes with proper attention and practice, though some people are never able to let themselves go enough to achieve it. Soften your gaze (allow it to go out of focus) and look into the water. Watch in a calm, detached way. See the moon and clouds in the water. They may seem to illuminate the bowl. Images may begin to form, pictures or symbols. Accept any images that come into your mind.

MAKING A SCRYING MIRROR

Find a piece of round concave glass (an old clock face, for example). Paint it black on the back (you may need several coats of paint). Keep it in the darkness, as it is to be used for a moon scrying mirror. Use it as previously described.

CHARGE YOUR CRYSTALS

The light of the full moon can be used to charge crystals to be used for moon magic and psychic work. Select only crystals associated with the moon and water. It is not suitable for charging crystals such as sunstone, tiger's eye, and so on that resonate with the sun. Cleanse them in running water (be careful as some, like selenite, will dissolve in water) or incense. Place them outside on your garden altar or a windowsill where the moonlight will reach them. Bring them in in the morning and wrap in a black cloth until you need them.

FULL MOON SELF-HEALING RITUAL

Perform outdoors, if you can, or otherwise at your altar on the night of the full moon. Think about your intent to be whole and healthy. You will need the following:

BOWL OF EARTH

FEATHER

CANDLE

CUP OF WATER

Open your sacred space. Light a silver or white candle. Call on the full moon goddess by whatever name you know her,

Lady [name], pregnant with all possibilities
Mother of stars, pearl of the night
I bathe in your radiance
And ask you for healing.

Take up the bowl of earth and pass it through the sign of the pentacle (i.e., draw an imaginary pentacle in the air with it). Say:

Moonlight on earth, may I be whole and well.

Take up the feather and pass it through the sign of the pentacle. Say:

Moonlight on the air, may I be mentally strong.

Take up the candle and pass it through the sign of the pentacle. Say:

Moonlight on the fire, may I have bountiful energy.

Take up the cup of water and pass it through the sign of the pentacle. Say:

Moonlight on the water, may I be emotionally whole.

Allow the cup of water to absorb the light of the moon. Say,

May I be whole and well!
May I be whole and well!
May I be whole and well!

Drink the water. Visualise the light of the moon flooding your body, absorbed into every cell. When you are ready, say,

> *Lady* [name]
> *Your light flows through me*
> *And calls all good things to me:*
> *Health, love, and abundance.*
> *Mother Moon, pearl of the night*
> *Light my path and guide my way.*
> *I honour and bless you, and give you my thanks.*
> *This rite is ended, blessed be.*

Close your sacred space.

DIVINATION TOOL CONSECRATION

Consecrate tools of divination, such as scrying mirrors, tarot cards, and runes, under the full moon. Cleanse the tool with frankincense smoke to remove any residual psychic energy absorbed from the shop or market they were bought from.

Under the light of a full moon, lay out the tools where they can receive the light of the moon. You will need

> BOWL OF EARTH
>
> WHITE CANDLE
>
> INCENSE
>
> CUP OF WATER

Light the incense and candle. Take the tool to be consecrated and face the east, hold it up to the moon for a few moments, then pass it over the incense and say,

> *Moon on air, I consecrate this* [mirror, tarot deck, etc.]
> *And charge it with your energies*
> *To give it power and make it sacred*
> *To aid me in my work.*

Take the tool and face the south, hold it up to the moon for a few moments, then pass it above the candle flame and say,

> *Moon on fire, I consecrate this* [mirror, tarot deck, etc.]
> *And charge it with your energies*

To give it power and make it sacred
To aid me in my work.

Take the tool and face the west, hold it up to the moon for a few moments, then pass it over the water and say,

Moon on water, I consecrate this [mirror, tarot deck, etc.]
And charge it with your energies
To give it power and make it sacred
To aid me in my work.

Take the tool and face the north, hold it up to the moon for a few moments, then pass it over the bowl of earth and say,

Moon on earth, I consecrate this [mirror, tarot deck, etc.]
And charge it with your energies
To give it power and make it sacred
To aid me in my work.
I charge this [mirror, tarot deck, etc.] by the power of the old Gods
By the power of the moon and stars
Consecrated, blessed be.

Use the newly consecrated tool as soon as possible.

Full Moon Gardening

At the full moon, growth above soil reaches its peak. The concentration of active ingredients in herbs and plants is highest at the full moon, when they should be picked. Yule trees that are felled on the traditional day—the third day before the eleventh full moon of the year—will keep their needles longer than those felled later.

Waning Moon Magic

The waning moon belongs to the crone moon goddess. Just as the energy of the moon ebbs and starts to draw inward, the magic of the waning moon is concerned with diminishing and winding down, letting go of bad habits and negative thinking, purification, banishing, and cleansing magic, including house cleansing.

RITUAL OF RELINQUISHING

This is a ritual to let go of that which no longer serves you—this can be a bad habit, a relationship, and so on. You will need the following:

> BLACK CANDLE
>
> RELINQUISHING OIL (PAGE 80)
>
> SHEET OF PAPER
>
> PEN WITH BLACK INK
>
> CAULDRON (OR FIREPROOF POT)
>
> MATCHES

Create your sacred space. Say,

> *Crone goddess of the waning moon*
> *I call upon you, lady of silence*
> *Goddess of shadows*
> *In your realm*
> *All things pass into darkness and death.*

Anoint the black candle with relinquishing oil, light it, and say,

> *This is the time of winding down*
> *Of relinquishing all that is no longer good and beneficial.*
> *I call on the crone to witness that:*
> *I release the past*
> *I release pain*
> *I release fear*
> *I release guilt*
> *I release limiting beliefs*
> *Crone goddess, I call on your aid*
> *As I release the old and embrace the new.*

Take the sheet of paper, write down what you want to relinquish, and say,

> *Lady, witness what I banish*
> *I willingly offer it to you, lady*
> *Take it into your realm*
> *With the waning moon, may it diminish and be gone.*

Burn the paper in the cauldron, visualising what you wish to be rid of being burned away. When it is fully burned, say,

> *Lady, you give release to what is weary and spent*
> *But the wheel of time spins on*
> *And from endings come new beginnings*
> *And this is your wisdom.*
> *Thank you for the lessons of this night.*
> *Blessed be.*

Allow the candle to burn out. For more waning moon cleansing and purification rituals, see part 1.

WANING MOON GARDENING

As Mother Earth breathes in with the waning moon, her receptivity increases. Strenuous physical work is easier now than during a waxing moon and any injuries sustained by over-doing it will heal quicker. This is a good time to prune trees and shrubs—they will "bleed" less and recover quickly. It is also a good time to weed and hoe to banish unwanted plants and pests. The energies of the waning moon are good for root crops. Sow root vegetables such as carrots and turnips just after the full moon, along with lettuce, which seems to respond better to waning moon energies. Do not sow flowers at this time. Do not plant anything in the week before the new moon. Cleaning out the greenhouse and clearing beds is best done at the waning moon.

Dark Moon Magic

For three days, the moon is swallowed by darkness and belongs to the dark mother. But just as all life generates in the darkness of the womb or seeds in the dark earth, during this dark phase, the moon mystically regenerates itself and begins life anew; within the darkness, all potentials are contained. This is the time of the dark mother, whose mystical power is endless. The days of the dark moon are good for deep inner journeys; now is not the time to act, but to retreat, think, and meditate. You may find that your dreams and intuitions are very powerful at this time; the otherworld may be trying to break through with small signs and unexpected encounters that you should take note of.

TRANSFORMATION RITUAL

You will need:

CAULDRON (OR LARGE FIREPROOF DISH)

TWO BLACK CANDLES

SMALL WHITE CANDLE (IN THE CAULDRON)

Say,

Dark mother of the moon, I call
Grandmother, teacher
Storyteller and lore keeper
Mistress of the cauldron
Of inspiration
Of manifestation
Of transformation
Of initiation
Dark mother of the moon, I call.

Light the black candles and say,

Dark mother
Your celestial womb
Gives birth to itself
Endlessly becoming;
Re-creating yourself in each moment.

Go to the cauldron, light the candle within it, and say,

Dark mother
Your womb is the dark void
That holds the seed of all potentials
You are the beginning and the end and the beginning once again
May I glimpse eternity
And know the inner light.

Meditate on this for a while. Say,

We are the grandmothers and teachers
We are the storytellers and lore keepers

Constantly transforming
Constantly manifesting
Constantly becoming
Dark mother, teach us.

Draw a tarot card or rune. Consider its lessons. When you are ready, say,

Dark mother of the moon,
Grandmother, teacher
Storyteller and lore keeper
Mistress of the cauldron
Of inspiration
Of manifestation
Of transformation
Of initiation
Dark mother of the moon, I acknowledge your gifts
And give thanks.
This rite is ended. Blessed be.

Dark Moon Retreat

Sometimes we need to retreat, be silent, and relax, to prepare ourselves for changes to come. In the darkness, the path of inner knowing is illuminated. This is a time to rest and be passively open to the unconscious influence of the otherworld and growth that is slow and unforced.

Prepare a dark, quiet place where you can sit comfortably. You can lie down if you wish. Have a single candle only, well shaded. Say,

I call upon you, dark lady of midnight
You are the keeper of darkness
The place of wisdom.
You are the keeper of silence
Where the voice of the soul is heard.
You are the keeper of stories
The knowledge of the ancestors.

You are the keeper of dreams
Where all realms entwine.
Let me wake to the dream

Sit or lie in meditation. It doesn't matter whether you fall asleep, as your dreams will be teaching dreams.

Dark Moon Dream Pillow

Take advantage of the power of your sleeping dreams by creating a vision sleep pillow.

> MUSLIN BAG
>
> 1 PART MUGWORT
>
> 1 PART HOPS
>
> 1 PART PASSIONFLOWER
>
> 1 PART CLARY SAGE

Fill the muslin bag with your dried herbs and place it beneath your own pillow as you sleep. Have a pen and notebook beside your bed so that you can write your dream down as you wake.

Dark Moon Divination

Divination at this time is performed to give you insights into the deepest mysteries. It is not done lightly. You can use your favourite divination tools (tarot, runes, scrying mirror). Drink a psychic tea, such as blue lotus, mugwort, or clary sage. Light a black candle and divination incense. Say,

Dark mother, goddess of deepest night
Keeper of secrets
Of thrice-spun threads of time
Cast aside your misty veil
And grant to me the sight.

Continue to perform your divination.

Dark Moon Gardening

If possible, do no work in the garden during the dark moon.

· · · · ·

Blue Moon

A blue moon is a second full moon in a calendar month. It is coincidence of the artificial calendar and has no resonance in the natural cycle or natural magic.

The Weather Witch

The moon is a weather witch; she predicts the weather. The cunning folk had many sayings and omens of the appearance of the moon affecting the weather:

A ring around the moon, rain comes soon.

If the moon shows a silver shield, be not afraid to sow your field. But if she rises haloed round, soon we'll walk on deluged ground.

When the moon lies on her back, then the sou'west wind will crack. When she rises up and nods, chill nor'easters dry the sods.

In the wane of the moon, a cloudy morning bodes a fair afternoon.

If the crescent moon holds its points upward, able to contain water, it predicts a dry spell. If the new moon stands on its points, expect rain to spill out.

A winter full moon is a time for long cold snaps.

A full moon in April brings frost.

A pale full moon indicates rain, while a red one brings wind.

A Christmas full moon predicts a poor harvest.

The days following a new moon or a full moon are typically stormy.

The moon with a circle brings water in her beak.

A new moon with sharp horns threatens windy weather.

Part Five
Operative Witchcraft

Though spells are the first thing a beginner looks for, there is an important reason why this part of the path is taught only after the rest has been explored and experienced. The first and most important kind of magic we use is to change ourselves, for spiritual growth and to honour the Gods; for this, we use ritual and living with intent to make our connections with the sacred. However, there is a second kind of magic we perform, which is to change things in the physical world, and we call this operative witchcraft. After all, the old wise women were practical people who midwifed babies, laid out the dead, and offered cures for ills, but those cures often came with a charm to make the spirit whole. They also performed spells for practical purposes, such as finding stolen goods or removing ill luck. Magic is the essence of being a witch, and spells are part of that magic, but *only* part. There is a reason the other kind of magic is taught and practiced first—you need to be aware that all magic changes you, for good or ill.

Magic is not the art of creating something out of nothing. The spiritual and the physical are intertwined, and one can affect the other. The performance of magic relies on a direct connection between the spirit in you and the spirit in the resources you work with—the stones, crystals, metals, plants, and so on. The physical part of the magic—the herbs, candles, and stones you might use—provide the focus and anchor of the spell and do have their own energies, but the real magic comes with the intent, preparation, visualisation, and charging. Just wishing is not magic. Why would you limit yourself to the power of your little wishes, when you can call upon the power of the sun and moon, stone and water, green kin and animal kin, the earth and the sky? Magic involves your whole being—the mind that considers the intent and designs the spell, the body that performs the practical part, and the spirit that empowers it in combination with the power of your ingredients.

Spells do work, as long as they are carefully prepared and performed with a clear intent and properly charged. When they don't work, it may be because one of these things is neglected or miscalculated, or because the magic tries to push too far against the natural flow of events. The funny thing about magic is that it always seems to give you what you need, not what you think you want. If you perform a spell to win the lottery, for example, it almost certainly won't work. But if you are desperate for money to pay your rent and have tried every honest means of getting it, a money spell may turn up a few lost banknotes in the pocket of an old jacket or down the back of the sofa, or perhaps an unexpected gift from a distant aunt. If you wanted to cast a love spell, you may ask that love might come to you in a general way, but never seek to manipulate someone with magic. Spells are cast for power, never power over, and if you practice such dark magic, you will be corrupted by it.

Operative witchcraft affects the material world. People sometimes say that magic is a neutral force, but when you cast a spell, you shape it into a very particular energy (healing, love, abundance, anger, hatred, vengeance, etc.) and put yourself in direct contact with that energy. This is why cursing and hexing can prove dangerous to the caster, as well as the recipient. All actions have consequences for good or ill, and magical acts are not exempt. There is an old Chinese proverb that when you seek revenge, you should dig two graves—one for the recipient of your malice, and one for yourself.

Rarely a week goes by when I don't get a message from someone suffering from the effects of a misjudged spell or being afraid of what they have set in motion. My friend and fellow witch Pamela Mitchell is a specialist ward and charm maker, and she told me that the two most asked for items from newbies are something to attract money and power, and something to get revenge. She points people to items to help earn money and protective items against harmful vibes, but she once had to explain to someone that calling on Nemesis, the goddess of justice, to demand "justice" would put them in the firing line to be checked out for their own misdeeds! Dangerous territory indeed.[12]

And there is one final thing you should remember. Magic is energy, and energy is never destroyed. It does not last a few days or weeks then fizzle out. It reverberates outward, like ripples moving out from a stone thrown into a pond. Magic has consequences that continue to reverberate for a very, very long time. There is no time limit on a spell unless you put one on. No spell should have an ending that includes the word *forever* or any similar expression. In magic, *forever* means exactly that. Imagine doing a love spell that binds you forever to someone you really like and then you go off him. Getting him out of your hair could prove extremely difficult. He could pester you for life. Both of you would be unhappy. You could then find he pops up in your next life and the one after that. You did say forever!

---

12 Pamela Mitchell, personal communication.

CHAPTER 16

· · · · · · · · · · · · · · · ·

Spells

Spells do not have to be complicated or involve many exotic ingredients. In fact, the more complicated the spell is, the more things there are to go wrong. You can use the ingredients you find in your immediate environment, which was the way of the old wise women, and these herbs, stones, feathers, shells, and so on will be far more effective in your spells than something you have bought off a shelf, because they resonate with what is close to you, and you will have sought and chosen them with care and intent.

Intent

Magic is never performed for its own sake, but always has a very specific, closely defined purpose to *change* something. You have to be very clear what the intention of the spell/ritual is and express it unambiguously. Anything open to misinterpretation will be misinterpreted; because magic, like water, always seeks the easiest course to the sea.

Spells *change* things, so never cast a spell to keep something the same. For example, if you have a partner who loves you, don't cast a spell to keep them. The spell will alter the flow of energies and may disrupt the relationship.

When preparing to cast a spell, you need to think very carefully about what the intention of it is and how you want it to manifest. For example, if it is a spell of healing, you want the recipient to be whole and well, and everything to work toward this in a positive way. You never bring the negative aspects into the spell—what you don't want—as the spell would amplify those things, so you would not say, "May Auntie Joan be free from cancer," as you are bringing the energy of cancer into the spell and magnifying it. You might say, "May Auntie Joan be whole and well."

An essential part of the preparation is the cultivation of a positive state of mind; you must believe that you can and will succeed. Your state of mind when working the magic affects the energy it puts out; if you go into it in a negative, confused, or angry state of mind, the magic magnifies these and reflects them back to you. If you are trying to do a spell for abundance and thinking about your poverty, the spell won't work—you must connect and surround yourself with the energy of abundance.

Preparation

This is about choosing the right time to perform the spell (the right season or phase of the moon) and getting everything ready. Choosing the physical ingredients (herbs, cords, candles, stones, etc.) that form the anchor of the spell and keep it present and manifesting. Each ingredient must be chosen for its inherent properties and magical correspondences to reinforce the intent and energy of the spell. For a healing spell, for example, you would choose herbs, symbols, and colours of healing and might decide to call upon gods of healing from your tradition. Conversely, if you use a lot of things with unsuitable energies, they can diffuse the spell before it has even started or send it completely off track; it's like putting salt into a pudding recipe instead of sugar. The pudding is going to be horrible. So, it is worth preparing your ingredients carefully. Remember that the more complicated you make it, and the more ingredients you use, the more potential there is for them not to gel together and for the spell to go wrong. Beware of overegging the pudding!

After this, you might compose a verse to chant while you mix and empower your spell. It doesn't have to rhyme (though this is traditional) and helps reinforce the idea that you are not speaking everyday words in an everyday context. These words help focus the magic. Remember that words have power, and it is important to get your words right and be specific. Consider the consequences that the wrong words might have, or the omission of necessary words. A friend of a friend set up a guardian spirit over a particular place but didn't give it a name. When the spellcaster died, the guardian spirit became troublesome, but because he had cast the spell without naming the guardian, no one could contact it and ask it to move on.

Visualisation

As each ingredient is assembled in the spell (adding ingredients to a scrip or bottle, for example), the intent is kept in mind, as well as the outcome you want. With our healing spell, you may say as you add each ingredient, "May Auntie Joan be whole and well," and visualise her shining with well-being. You should not allow your mind to wander to other things, particularly to the illness, as these will also become part of the spell.

Charging

This is the part of the spell that activates all the magic, holds it together, and starts it manifesting in the world. It is done by appealing to the higher forces—the Gods—for help, imbuing the physical anchor of the spell with what you desire as hard as you can and speaking the words of the spell, all the time concentrating on the desired outcome. Remember that the Gods and spirits are another level of vibrational energy and are not your servants and may not be interested in your whims. Wait until you are properly acquainted with any deity or energy before you start appealing to them for help in casting a spell—it is only polite, after all.

Afterward

Then you step away and leave the spell to work. When a ritual or spell does not seem to have immediate effects, the temptation is to perform another one. But once you put the pudding in the oven, you leave it alone—you don't keep opening the oven door to look at it or poke it around. The reality is that it may take months or longer for the results of a spell to work itself to you. If you keep working more spells for the same thing, you are necessarily putting out different energies each time and the energies become conflicting and chaotic. If the first spell is working, the second spell will often send it off course, because you have altered the instruction by word, deed, or the energy of the moment. Add a third to that and who knows what will happen. Resist any temptation to meddle with it and repeat it. This would be disastrous. It may take some time, don't expect immediate results, and unless you have been very specific, it may not happen in the way you want it to.

Wait until the spell has worked, then you can dismantle the object and bury any herbs, and so on, so that they may return to Mother Earth. Any crystals can be cleansed and reused.

Using Natural Objects

The old wise women and cunning men would use whatever the land supplied for magic. These found objects held a natural connection with the land, plants, and animals.

STONES AND PEBBLES

Have you ever found yourself attracted to a pebble you found on the beach? Did you take it home and wonder why? The hearth witch usually uses the rocks and pebbles she finds in her environment, rather than buying crystals that may have been ripped from Mother Earth in an environmentally destructive way. (If you do use crystals, make sure they come from an ethical source.)

Like individual plants, different stones have distinct energies we can tap into, ranging from the sharp rocks of a mountainside to the quartz-striped garden pebble, colourful beach pebbles, and smooth river stones, which carry the memory of land and water, or flints, which hold the hidden power of fire within them.

Stones are the bones of Mother Earth, and through them we can connect to her. Meditating with a stone can help you connect with Mother Earth and ages past. They hold the memory of the land.

You can use a stone to represent the goddess on your altar. In some cultures, the goddess was represented by a rock or stone. In Phrygia, for example, rather than an anthropomorphic statue, the goddess Cybele was represented by a black unshaped stone, while in Cyprus, the goddess Aphrodite was worshipped in the form of an aniconic black stone.

Stones have a permeance that plants and animals do not. The pebble you hold in your hand may have been sitting in its environment for thousands of years. Stones teach us the value of rootedness and being grounded. Hold a stone and reflect on this whenever you feel ungrounded.

Stones and fossils may be used in spells, wards, or as amulets:

AMMONITE: helps open your path

FAIRY LOAVES (FOSSILISED SEA URCHINS): protects the hearth and oven

HAGSTONE (NATURALLY HOLED STONE): protection

LODESTONE: protection from disease, attracts luck and money

SHEPHERD'S CROWNS (FOSSILISED SEA URCHINS): the natural fivefold pattern keeps away evil

THUNDERSTONE (FOSSILISED BELEMNITE): puts you under the protection of the thunder god

Finally, consider making a circle of pebbles for your rituals, surrounding you with the energy and memory of the earth.

Prayer to the Stone Mother

> *Ancient one, eternal mother of time*
> *Bone of the mother*
> *I hold aeons in my hand*
> *You endure forever*
> *I connect to the past through you.*

BONES

If I see the weathered bones and skulls of animals and birds on my outings, I am often drawn to them. They are the physical remains of a creature that once walked the land, holding a memory of a life lived and a spirit passed on.

You can use bones, claws, and teeth to forge a link and connect to animal spirits. The skull of a red deer, for example, carries the genetic memory of the whole species, and you might use it to connect to the spirit of red deer. If you have a fox spirit familiar, you might use the bones or teeth of a fox to strengthen your connection to it. If used regularly, the bone can become a spirit vessel for your fox familiar.

Bones, horns, teeth, and claws might be used in a spell (perhaps incorporated into a scrip or bottle) to add the power of the animal species to it—the cunning of a fox, the strength of a boar, and so on. You can also use them in meditation to call on their qualities when you need them.

Some witches use bones, horns, and antlers when making magical tools. I have a knife with a ram's horn handle. Others just use the bone or horn itself as a tool in ritual. I have a set of shed antlers on my altar to represent the horned god.

We never kill or harm any creature to take items for magic. Apart from being morally indefensible, the pain and anger the animal feels at its untimely death will always live in the bones and corrupt any spell.

FEATHERS

Not everyone might be attracted to bones, but I'm pretty sure that we've all picked up feathers we've found. For magic, always use natural feathers you have found yourself, never bought ones, and never dyed ones.

Feathers have played a part in magic, myth, and folklore since the dawn of history. The ancients believed that birds could visit the realm of the Gods in their flight and might in turn be messengers from the spirit world. Finding a feather often seems significant to us.

Feathers naturally belong to the element of air. The powers of air are concerned with the intellect, the powers of the mind, knowledge (as opposed to wisdom), logic, inspiration, information, teaching, memory, thought, and communication.

Feathers may be used in spells and rituals of communication and connection, whether to the spirit realm or beings on this plane. This includes rituals of spirit flight.

You can use a large feather as a fan to disperse incense or ritual fumigations around the working area.

Feathers that are significant to you can be added to wands, staffs, witch's ladders, wards, scrips, and witch bottles for magical work.

Think about the kind of feather you intend to add to a spell. It is traditional to use the feathers of the gentle dove in a love spell, for example, the feathers of the sharp-eyed hawk in a ritual for far sight, a crow feather for prophecy and divination, or an owl feather for wisdom, but don't be too caught up in lists of bird correspondences—the situation you found a feather in may tell you what it is for.

SHELLS

We find seashells on the shore, the liminal space between land and sea, a hidden place only uncovered when the tide recedes, revealing its mysteries and gifts.

In classical myth, seashells were attributes of Venus/Aphrodite, who was born from the churning of sea-foam (*aphros* in Greek) when Cronos cut off the genitals of the sky god Uranus and threw them into the sea. Rising from the waves, Aphrodite, goddess of love, sailed on a seashell to the island of Cyprus. Shells were thought to resemble female genitalia, or the womb, and represent the feminine, fertility, and abundance, birth and rebirth. They connect us with the ocean, that abundant womb from which all life emerged, and can be used in rituals and spells of fertility and love.

If you hold a shell up to your ear, you can hear the ocean, and it is always connected to its source and the magic of water—flowing, nourishing, love, cleansing, the emotions, compassion and empathy, harmony and beauty. You can place a shell on your altar to represent the element of water or use a large shell to hold liquids during a ritual. For rituals and spells of cleansing and purification, water can be poured from a shell onto the object or person being cleansed.

For workings designed to promote peace and serenity, seashells can be used as a focus for meditation.

Add small shells to scrips and witch bottles for spells of prosperity, fertility, and abundance. Carry a shell or make one into a necklace as a natural amulet to attract good fortune. Make a wind chime of shells and hang it outside your door to attract plenty.

Spell Anchors

There are many things that may be used as the physical anchor to your spell, from bottles and scrips, to shells and stones. These are just a few.

WITCH BOTTLES

Historical witch bottles were used for protection, but witch bottles can be used as anchors for other kinds of spells. You might make a witch bottle for abundance, one to attract love, and so on. You will need a glass or pottery wide-necked bottle or jar, suitable herbs, crystals, and symbols for your purpose.

Witch Bottle for Abundance

At the waxing moon, clear your mind and clarify your intent.

GLASS OR CERAMIC BOTTLE OR JAR

COINS (WEALTH)

SEASHELL (PROSPERITY)

BASIL (RESONATES WITH THE FLOW OF ABUNDANCE)

CLOVES (MONEY DRAWING)

DATE (PLENTY)

SUNFLOWER SEEDS (LUCK, INCREASE)

GREEN WAX

Concentrate on your intent as you put each ingredient in the bottle. Say something like,

May abundance flow into my life.

Perhaps you might appeal to gods of wealth, such as Ops, the Roman goddess of plenty, whose name means "riches" (or another deity from your own tradition). Say something like,

Ops, goddess of plenty, may abundance flow into my life in all its forms.

Seal the jar with wax. Once assembled, you simply keep the bottle where you can see it to remind you what you are working on.

Witch Bottle to Attract Friendship

On a waxing moon, clear your mind and clarify your intent.

GLASS OR CERAMIC BOTTLE OR JAR

GREEN MOSS AGATE (TO WIN NEW FRIENDS)

LAPIS LAZULI (TO BUILD FRIENDSHIPS)

CATMINT (TO ATTRACT FRIENDSHIP)

OREGANO (FOR HAPPY RELATIONSHIPS)

PASSIONFLOWER (TO INCREASE YOUR POPULARITY)

PINK WAX

Concentrate on your intent as you put each ingredient in the bottle, saying something like,

May friendship and fellowship flow into my life.

Perhaps you might appeal to Gods of friendship and hospitality, such as the hearth goddess Vesta. Say something like,

Vesta, goddess of who keeps the welcoming hearth, may friendship and good fellowship come to my hearth.

Seal the jar with wax. Once assembled, you simply keep the bottle near your hearth where you can see it to remind you what you are working on.

Witch Bottle for Fertility

At the waxing moon, clear your mind and clarify your intent.

GLASS OR CERAMIC BOTTLE OR JAR

UNAKITE (FOR ABUNDANCE AND NURTURING)

CARNELIAN (PROMOTES SEXUAL HEALTH)

1 ALMOND (FOR REGENERATION)

PIECE OF BIRCH BARK (FOR NEW BEGINNINGS)

1 DATE (FOR THE GODDESS OF FERTILITY)

PINECONE (FOR THE GOD OF FERTILITY)

9 SUNFLOWER SEEDS (FOR BLESSINGS)

SEASHELL (FERTILITY, SYMBOLIC OF REPRODUCTIVE SYSTEM)

GREEN WAX

Concentrate on your intent as you put each ingredient in the bottle, saying something like,

Fertile and fruitful.

Perhaps you might appeal to gods of fertility, such as Demeter. Saying something like,

Demeter, goddess of fertility, bless me with your powers.

Seal the jar with wax. Once assembled, keep the bottle in your bedroom or under your bed.

SCRIPS

A scrip is a small pouch or bag filled with dried herbs, gemstones, and symbols, or scrips can be filled with dried herbs alone. Some modern witches call them charm bags. You can either buy a pouch or, better still, make one yourself. It doesn't have to be a work of art; it is the intent that is important. You will need an oblong piece of cloth, big enough to take all the ingredients when folded in half and sewn up. Choose a sturdy fabric, and the right colour adds extra strength to the magic. Take the cloth and fold it in half, right sides together. Sew up three sides, reinforcing your intent with each stitch (you can chant it as you sew), and then turn it right side out. Clear your mind and concentrate on your intent. Put the ingredients into the scrip one by one, stating your desire each time. Sew it shut (or bind it with thread, which enables you to knot in the magic), calling upon a relevant deity you work with for help. Then carry it with you, put it in the appropriate room of your house, or sleep with it under your pillow, according to its purpose.

Personal Power Scrip

To reinforce your personal power, gather things that present themselves to you at places and times of power—feathers, stones, shells, plant material such as twigs, roots, seeds, or pieces of bark, bones, teeth or claws, beads, and feathers. These are sacred objects, discovered in a sacred way—objects that have spiritual meaning for you. You can put them all in the scrip at the same time or add additional items that present themselves to you.

If the scrip is small enough, you can carry it with you at all times, or just when you need to draw on the power of its components for strength and protection.

Prosperity Drawing Scrip

Assemble at the waxing moon.

GREEN SCRIP

GREEN THREAD

3 ALMONDS (FERTILITY, BLOSSOMING, INCREASE)

PINCH OF CINNAMON POWDER (DRAWS POSITIVE ENERGY)

3 CLOVES (LUCK, MONEY)

3 SAGE LEAVES (WISHES, ABUNDANCE)

OATS (WEALTH)

As you place each ingredient into the bag, say,

Abundance and prosperity flow throughout the universe, flow to me.

Tie up the scrip with the green thread. Hold it in your strongest hand and say,

Gods of prosperity [you can name a deity you work with here], *I have prepared this charm so that prosperity may flow to me in ways that are good and needful. I charge this charm with love and abundance. So mote it be.*

You can place the charm in your handbag or in the cash register of your business.

Healing Sun Scrip

This charm calls upon the god of sun and healing. You can name the sun god (or goddess) according to your tradition.

YELLOW SCRIP

GOLD THREAD

2 TEASPOONS BAY LEAVES (FOR THE SUN GOD)

2 TEASPOONS CHAMOMILE FLOWERS (RENEWAL)

PINCH CINNAMON POWDER (ENERGISING AND HEALING)

2 TEASPOONS MARIGOLD PETALS (PROTECTION)

2 TEASPOONS ROSEMARY LEAVES (FOR CLEARING DISEASE)

PIECE OF AMBER (FOR HEALING AND CLEANSING THE BODY)

At noon, Ostara, or Midsummer, clear your mind and concentrate on your intent, place the amber in the bag, then sprinkle in the herbs, saying,

> *Golden god of the sun and healing*
> *I call upon you to lend me your power*
> *And bless this healing charm.*
> *Imbue it with your strength and energy*
> *So that it shall heal and restore me.*
> *Blessed be.*

Tie up the bag with the gold thread and keep it near you.

Scrip for Inner Peace

Healing is not just about the body, but also concerns the mind and spirit.

PINK SCRIP

PINK THREAD

2 TEASPOONS LAVENDER FLOWERS (PEACE)

2 TEASPOONS CHAMOMILE FLOWERS (TRANQUILLITY)

2 TEASPOONS PINK ROSE PETALS (LOVE AND HARMONY)

2 TEASPOONS OLIVE LEAVES (PEACE)

FEW DROPS MELISSA OIL (JOY)

PIECE OF ROSE QUARTZ (CALM AND PEACE)

At the waxing moon, lay out a circle of pink cloth and sprinkle the herbs on its centre, saying,

> *Concordia [or god/goddess of peace from your tradition]*
> *I blend this herbal charm*
> *To bring me inner peace.*
> *To bring me tranquillity*
> *Goddess, bless this charm*
> *And bring me inner strength.*

· · · · ·

Add the rose quartz and tie up the parcel with the pink thread. Keep it near you and rub it when you need its power.

Peace in the Home Scrip

Assemble at the full moon.

> BLUE SCRIP
>
> PIECE OF ANGELICA ROOT (PROTECTION)
>
> 2 TEASPOONS DRIED CHAMOMILE FLOWERS (CALM)
>
> 2 TEASPOONS DRIED LAVENDER FLOWERS (LOVE)
>
> 2 TEASPOONS DRIED LEMON VERBENA (PEACE, JOY, COMMUNICATION)
>
> 3 OLIVE LEAVES (PEACE)
>
> 1 TEASPOON SANDALWOOD BARK OR POWDER (TRANQUILLITY)
>
> SMALL ROSE QUARTZ CRYSTAL (PEACE AND CALM)

Say these words:

> *Hearth goddess, I call upon you*
> *You who dwells within the home*
> *May there be peace in my home*
> *May there be love*
> *May there be joy*
> *May all be heard.*

Place it in the kitchen or sitting room.

Home Protection Scrip

Assemble at the full moon.

> WHITE CLOTH
>
> RED THREAD
>
> 1 ACORN (PROTECTION)
>
> PIECE OF ANGELICA ROOT (PROTECTION)
>
> 3 BAY LEAVES (BANISHING NEGATIVITY)
>
> A PINCH OF DRIED CALENDULA PETALS (LOVE AND PROTECTION)
>
> 3 HOLLY LEAVES (PROTECTION)

9 ROWANBERRIES (BANISHING NEGATIVITY)

A PINCH OF DRIED VERVAIN (CLEANSING AND PROTECTION)

Say these words:

> Hearth goddess, I call upon you
> You who dwells within the home
> Protect this place
> And all within it.

Place it in your porch or kitchen or in the highest part of the house.

Full Moon Fertility Scrip

At the full moon, place each ingredient inside the pouch.

GREEN SCRIP

GREEN THREAD

SEASHELL (FERTILITY)

3 ALMONDS (FERTILITY, BLOSSOMING, INCREASE)

3 GRAINS BARLEY (FERTILITY, ABUNDANCE)

3 VIOLET FLOWERS (LOVE)

2 WALNUT HALVES (FERTILITY, WISHES GRANTED)

3 ACORNS (FERTILITY, GROWTH)

3 SUNFLOWER SEEDS (FERTILITY, BLESSINGS, ABUNDANCE)

3 GRAINS RICE (FERTILITY AND BLESSINGS)

3 RED ROSE PETALS (LOVE)

Say,

> Lady Moon, hear me.
> Fertile mother, with your pregnant belly
> Look down on me and witness my desire
> Share your abundance with me
> Let me be filled with life

Place it under your pillow or under the bed.

Love Drawing Scrip

Make at the waxing moon.

PINK CLOTH

DRIED PEEL OF ONE APPLE (LOVE)

7 DRIED BASIL LEAVES (LOVE AND HARMONY)

HALF A CINNAMON STICK (PASSION)

3 CLOVES (LOVE, WARMTH)

7 DRIED RED ROSE PETALS (LOVE)

1 VANILLA POD (HAPPINESS)

Say,

Goddess of love
Witness that I draw love to me
By the power of these herbs
By the power of my will
By the power of your blessings.
Witness and grant my desire.

Carry it close to your heart.

Knot Magic

In everyday life, we use knots to tie up and bind physical things—we tie our shoelaces, bind a plant onto a trellis, or wrap up a parcel. In just the same way, for magic, we use knots to bind nonphysical things or trap harmful intentions. Witches have always used knots to contain illness, secure love, confine evil spirits, weave blessings, control the weather, and bind curses; it's an ancient magic. Long ago, in Egypt, Isis, the powerful goddess of magic, knotted, spun, and wove her spells, weaving or knotting various forces to control them. She taught the art of using magical knots.

The tying of a knot denotes the binding of a spell, while the untying of a knot represents releasing the magic or breaking the enchantment. The old sea witches would sell sailors knotted bags of wind, who, when they need a breeze, could release one of the knots.

You can use string, hair, ribbon, or wool and tie knots into it, saying your words of power. Different coloured cords can be used, enabling the resonance of colour magic to be incorporated, with several cords of different colours knotted together. Remember that knotting, weaving, and braiding symbolise the bringing together of disparate elements and binding them together.

NINE-KNOT MAGIC

The simplest form of knot magic is to tie nine knots in a cord, alternating them from each end and working toward the centre, concentrating on what it is you wish to achieve, tying it into the knot. It is best to do this at a waxing moon. There are many variations of the accompanying chant:

> By the knot of one, the spell's begun
> By the knot of two, the power come true
> By the knot of three, so mote it be
> By the knot of four, my will be law
> By the knot of five, the spell's alive
> By the knot of six, the magic fix
> By the knot of seven, my words to heaven
> By the knot of eight, I bind up fate
> By the knot of nine, this thing be mine.

Put the cord somewhere safe and leave it as long as you wish the spell to work. When you wish to undo the spell, undo or cut the knots.

WAXING MOON LOVE KNOT

This is a spell to draw love to you. Perform at the waxing moon. Take a red cord. Light a love incense (page 79). Say,

> Dance the circle dance of dreaming
> Lonely by the crystal sea
> Spin the web of mist and moonlight
> Come, beloved, and follow me.

Tie the first knot in the red cord. Say,

> Chant the chant of souls entwining
> Round and through the scared fire
> Drink from wells of mist and moonshine
> Lover, come to love's desire.

Tie the second knot. Say,

> *Dream the dream of solemn passion*
> *Through the star encrusted night*
> *Weave the web of mist and moonfire*
> *Loved one, know all love's delight.*

Tie the third knot. Say,

> *Hear the tides, the heaving waters*
> *Sombre on the crystal sand*
> *Hear the chant of longing, waiting*
> *Come, fulfil at love's demand.*

Tie the fourth knot. Say,

> *Seek and love my waiting body*
> *Waiting nightly by the sea*
> *Tread the path of mist and moonlight*
> *Lover, come beloved to me.*[13]

Tie the fifth knot. Place the cord on your altar or in another safe place.

Witch's Ladder

Though they have no historical antecedents, witch's ladders find appeal with today's witches, and witch's ladders have become widely used in the modern craft, sometimes for spells, sometimes for meditation, or sometimes like a rosary to keep count of repetitive chants.[14]

When you think of a ladder, it is something you climb to get you somewhere, so the spell builds with each item and knot you put into it. You could use different coloured cords

---

13 Traditional witches' chant.

14 Only one example of an historical witch's ladder has ever been recorded, donated to the Pitt Rivers Museum by the widow of anthropologist Edward Burnett Tylor. He was given the object, which was said to have been found in the attic of an old woman after she'd died. She was rumoured to be a witch, so the string knotted with cock feathers was immediately associated with witchcraft and thought to be used for stealing milk from cows (though very similar strings were used by countryfolk to scare birds and deer).

to suit the purpose of the spell, braiding as many as you think suitable—green for growth, orange for joy, red for passion, and so on. Charms, feathers, gemstones, twigs, herbs, bones, hair, shells, keys, and so on may be knotted into the cord, depending on the purpose of the spell—feathers to represent messages and the element of air, and gemstones according to their correspondences (amethyst for healing, rose quartz for peace, etc.).

Take your cords and knot them at one end. As you tie your knots and bind in your objects, chant your intent, storing it in every knot. When you have finished, tie off your cord. You might say something like,

> *God and goddess, so mote it be.*

Hang your ladder over your altar, or if it is for protection, you might want to hang it by the door or by your bed.

BEDROOM PROTECTION WITCH LADDER

Think about your intent of protecting your bedroom and yourself during the night.

> RED TWINE OR WOOL
>
> ACORN (FOR PROTECTION)
>
> ANCHOR CHARM (FOR STABILITY)
>
> SMALL BELL (DISPELS NEGATIVITY)
>
> HAZEL TWIG (PROTECTION)
>
> CINNAMON STICK (PROTECTION)
>
> DRIED LEMON SLICES (AGAINST THE EVIL EYE)
>
> CHILLI (PROTECTION, DISPELS NEGATIVITY)
>
> JASPER STONE (AGAINST NIGHTMARES)
>
> FLINT STONE (AGAINST NIGHTMARES)

All the components will be knotted onto the red twine during the course of the spell. You might need to wrap the stones and some other objects with silver wire to enable you to attach them. As each knot is made, a spell is spoken:

> *Hearth goddess, protect this place, and protect me.*

Hang your ladder to anchor this energy in place.

Ribbon Charms

I am indebted to my friend Pamela Mitchell, a dedicated charm maker, for inspiring me with this method of charm making. Her charms incorporate coloured ribbons (according to their colour correspondences), symbolic charms (such as shells, bones, feathers, jewellery, etc.), and knot magic. You can incorporate a piece of paper into the charm on which the spell is written.

Ribbon Charm for Emotional Healing

Gather the following items.

> Sea-blue ribbon (for water and the emotions)
>
> Indigo ribbon (for mental health)
>
> Red ribbon (for strength and courage)
>
> Gold ribbon (for the healing power of the sun god)
>
> Small piece of paper (to write the spell on)
>
> Blue ink and pen
>
> Piece of rose quartz (for calm and emotional healing)
>
> Gold coloured metal charm of the sun face (optimism)
>
> Butterfly jewellery charm (for transformation)
>
> Gold wire (for the power of the sun)

On a Sunday (the day of the sun), noon, at Midsummer, or during the waxing moon, take the pen and paper and write the spell on it:

> I *am strong, I am resilient, I am transformed.*

Roll the paper into a cylinder and wrap the wire around it, taking care to leave plenty of wire to attach the ribbons. As you wire in each object, you are binding the spell.

Take the first ribbon (sea blue for water and the emotions). Wrap the wire around one end to attach it to the paper cylinder, saying,

> I *flow like the sea and accept the tides of being.*

Take the second ribbon (indigo for emotional healing). Wrap the wire around one end to attach it to the paper cylinder, saying,

My emotions are strong and resilient. I am whole.

Take the third ribbon (red for strength and courage). Wrap the wire around one end to attach it to the paper cylinder, saying,

I am strong, I am courageous. I look forward to what will come.

Take the fourth ribbon (gold for optimism and the healing power of the sun). Wrap the wire around one end to attach it to the paper cylinder, saying,

I look forward with optimism. Good things will come to me.

Wire in the piece of rose quartz (for calm and emotional healing), saying,

I am calm, I open myself to peace and harmony.

Wire in the sun charm, saying,

The sun lightens all darkness. Father Sun, shine on me.

Attach the butterfly charm:

I transform myself and fly free.

Run your hand down each ribbon in turn, mentally throwing its powers before you into the future.

Hang the charm where you will see it every day.

Candle Magic

Candle magic is one of the easiest and most widespread forms of spellcasting.

The simplest method is to decide on the type of spell you wish to cast. Choose a suitable coloured candle and a suitable oil for your purpose. Set it up in a secure holder on your altar or on a low table one evening and put out most of the lights in the room. Anoint the candle middle to top and middle to bottom with the oil, concentrating on what you want to achieve. When you are satisfied, light the candle, saying,

By this candle's glowing light
May my magic pierce the night
By my will the spell be done
By this act my wish be won
Now I set this magic free
As I will so mote it be.

Leave it to burn itself out (make sure it is in a safe place). It is always best to use a small candle so you can keep an eye on it until it burns away.

Candle Colours

Here's a brief list of colour correspondences.

BLACK: banishing, repelling, death, endings, winding down

BLUE (LIGHT): tranquillity, peace, calm, harmony, protection, healing, justice, water, emotions

BROWN: stability, earthiness

GOLD: happiness, rejuvenation, strength, healing

GREEN: fertility, growth, prosperity, abundance, the earth and practical matters

GREY: communication, study, teaching, divination

INDIGO: perceptiveness, vision, intuition, insight, emotional healing

MAGENTA: vision, creativity, insight, inspiration

ORANGE: optimism, success, courage, bravery, luck

PINK: love, romance, friendship, happiness, harmony, peace, compassion

PURPLE: strength, mastery, power, protection

RED: life, vitality, energy, passion, strength, health, fire

SILVER: intuition, truth, enlightenment

TURQUOISE: philosophy, creativity, communication

VIOLET: spiritual healing, spiritual growth, self-esteem

WHITE: peace, cleansing, defensive magic, protection, purity, harmony, purification, tranquillity

YELLOW: strength of mind, learning, study, eloquence, joy, the element of air

CANDLE SPELL TO ATTRACT FRIENDSHIP

Gather the following items.

> 3 PINK CANDLES IN HOLDERS
>
> 10 MILLILITRES SUNFLOWER OIL
>
> 3 DROPS OREGANO ESSENTIAL OIL (JOY, HAPPINESS, FRIENDSHIP)
>
> 2 DROPS CARDAMOM ESSENTIAL OIL (ATTRACTION)
>
> 10-MILLILITRE GLASS BOTTLE
>
> DISH OF HONEY (OR HONEY SUBSTITUTE)
>
> DISH OF RAISINS
>
> DISH OF DATES

This spell invokes the Three Graces. According to Greek legend, after Aphrodite, the goddess of love, arose from the sea and arrived at Cyprus, the Three Graces bedecked her with golden ornaments and escorted her to the divine halls of Olympus. Her attendants are Thalia (Joy), Euphrosyne (Mirth), and Aglaea (Splendour), the three graces of life who bring friendship, fellowship, and joy to gods and men. They preside over all banquets, dances, and happy social events. Don't forget to honour them by whatever name you call such deities, for without love and friendship, fun, grace, beauty and art, all striving is meaningless, and the wonder of the world is lost.

On a Sunday or during a waxing moon, pour the sunflower oil into the glass bottle and add the essential oils. Shake the bottle, concentrating positively on your desire to attract friendship. Set up the candles and clear your mind, focus on your intent of attracting new friends in a positive way—visualise your goal, not your lack. Keep this in mind as you anoint the candles with the oil.

Light the first candle, saying,

> *Thalia, goddess, hear me. May there be joy in my life, may there be love and friendship and wonder at the beauty of creation.*

Taste the honey. Say,

> *May I know the sweetness of joy.*

Light the second candle, saying,

> *Euphrosyne, goddess, hear me. May there be mirth in my life, may there be laughter with friends.*

Taste the raisins. Say,

> *May I know the sweetness of mirth.*

Light the third candle, saying,

> *Aglaea, goddess, hear me. May there be splendour in my life, may there be beauty, grace, and creativity with friends.*

Taste the dates. Say,

> *May I know the sweetness of splendour. So mote it be.*

Allow the candles to burn out.

Casket

A casket (small box or chest) may be used to anchor a spell, and it is an alternative to a witch bottle. It may contain herbs, symbolic objects, crystals, and so on, according to the intent of the spell, and will keep them secure. The box, once filled, is charged and sealed (glued down, sealed with wax or screwed shut). It can be kept on the altar or some other place of your choosing. On a shelf, no one will know what it is, or what it is doing, so it can be quite a discreet form of magic.

Define the intent of your spell. Choose a suitable box. Collect all the ingredients you will need. As you place them in the box, visualise your intent. You might want to add a piece of paper with the spell written on it.

Speak your spell.

Close the box. Put it in your chosen storage space.

LOVE-DRAWING CASKET

Perform at the waxing moon.

> HEART-SHAPED BOX
>
> 7 ROSEBUDS (LOVE WILL BLOSSOM)

PIECE OF ROSE QUARTZ (HEART OPENER)

PAPER, PEN, AND RED INK

Take the pen and paper and write,

> *Goddess of love*
> *I call to you*
> *I draw love to me*
> *May love find its way to me.*
> *Goddess of love*
> *I call to you*
> *Grant my desire.*

Put the rose quartz and rosebuds into the box, visualising your intent. Finally, put the written spell into the box and say it out loud.

Seal the box and store it where you can see it every day.

Charms and Jewellery

As well as using colours, gems, and metals in your spells, you can incorporate symbols, either in the form of images, actual items (such as a key), or jewellery charms of the type that go onto charm bracelets and pendants. A charm bracelet is a collection of amulets grouped together.

ACORN: luck, prosperity

ANCHOR: security, stability

ARROW: direction, purpose

BAT: magic, enchantment

BEAR: strength, courage

BEE: community, industriousness

BELL: dispelling negativity

BIRD: freedom, perspective

BUTTERFLY: change, hope, transformation

CADUCEUS: healing, harmony

CAT: independence

CLADDAGH: love, loyalty

CLOVER (FOUR-LEAF): health, wealth, love, and respect

COIN: prosperity, wealth

COMPASS: direction

CORN: potential, fertility

CRESCENT MOON: transformation, change, growth

CROWN: power, triumph, glory

DAGGER: strength, protection

DEER: grace, beauty

DOG: fidelity, loyalty

DOLPHIN: harmony

DOVE: peace

DRAGON: power, wisdom, strength

DRAGONFLY: change, transformation

EAGLE: far sight

ELEPHANT: stability, luck, strength

EYE: protection

FISH: fertility, good luck, prosperity

FLOWER: growth, blossoming

FOX: cunning, wisdom, intelligence

FROG: regeneration, healing, cleansing

FULL MOON: intuition, clarity, wisdom

HAMMER: protection

HAND OF FATIMA: protection

HARE: fecundity

HEART: love

HEDGEHOG: wisdom

HORN: luck, protection

HORSE: strength, power, movement

HORSESHOE: luck, prosperity, protection

HUMMINGBIRD: joy

INFINITY SYMBOL: eternity, the cosmic whole

KEY: opening, unlocking

LADYBIRD (LADYBUG): luck, protection

LEAF: growth, youth

LIGHTNING BOLT: sudden illumination, destruction of ignorance

LION: courage, power, dignity, strength

LIZARD: healing, renewal

LOCK: security

LOTUS: purity, enlightenment

MERMAID: love, beauty, sensuality

MOUSE: abundance

MUSHROOM: sudden growth

OPEN UMBRELLA: protection

OWL: wisdom, foresight

OX: power, strength

OYSTER: protection

PEGASUS: spiritual aspiration

PENTAGRAM: protection

PIG: fecundity, abundance

RABBIT: birth, fertility

RAVEN: prophecy

ROSE: love, spiritual aspiration, beauty, passion

SAFETY PIN: joining

SCARAB: resurrection, protection

SCISSORS: cutting bonds

SEAHORSE: good luck

SKULL: death, mortality

SNAKE: fertility, rebirth, immortality, healing

SPIDER: creativity, connections

SPOON: love

STAR: courage, purity, dreams, guidance

SUN: healing, happiness, optimism, creativity, positive energy

SUNFLOWER: loyalty

SWALLOW: safety, security, renewal

SWAN: love, grace, union, partnership

TASSEL: protection, prestige, spiritual connection

TIGER: strength and self-confidence

TREE OF LIFE: family, link between heaven and earth, growth, strength

UNICORN: purity, innocence, enchantment

WATERING CAN: positive developments in your life

WHALE: balance, healing, strength

WISHBONE: good luck, wishes come true

WOLF: loyalty, generosity

WOOL, YARN: weaving of magic

· · · · ·

CHAPTER 17

· · · · · · · · · · · · ·

Spell Formulations

Here are some correspondences for various spell types.

Love Spells

PLANET: Venus

DAY: Friday

MOON: waxing or full

COLOUR: red or pink

GEMSTONES: emerald, star sapphire, lodestone, carbuncle, chalcedony, rose quartz, ruby

METAL: copper

HERBS: apple, basil, calendula, cardamom, carnation, catmint, cherry, cinnamon, clove, coriander, daisy, damiana, dittany of Crete, fig, frankincense, fuchsia, geranium, ginger, ginseng, goldenrod, gorse, honeysuckle, houseleek, jasmine, lavender, lemon balm, lily, linden, lovage, mallow, mandrake, meadowsweet, mistletoe, myrrh, nettle, orange, oregano, passionflower, pomegranate, poppy, primrose, rose, rosemary, saffron, sweet cicely, valerian, violet, yarrow

SYMBOLS: heart, claddagh, four-leaf clover, dove feather

DEITIES: Venus, Aphrodite, Eros, Cupid, Hathor, Bes, Parvati, Astarte, Inanna, Ishtar, Milda, Siebog, Ziva, Aine, Branwen, Freya, Frigg, Turan, Bangan, Yue-Lao

Friendship Spells

PLANET: sun

DAY: Sunday

MOON: waxing

COLOUR: pink

GEMSTONES: agate, rose quartz, tourmaline, lapis lazuli, topaz

METALS: gold, rose gold

HERBS: begonia, carnation, catmint, linden, oregano, passionflower

SYMBOLS: two-handled cup, interlocking hands, infinity symbol, knot

DEITIES: Mitra, Hestia, Vesta, the Three Graces, Concordia, Harmonia

Healing Spells

PLANET: sun

DAY: Sunday

MOON: waxing

COLOURS: gold (healing power of the sun), deep yellow (sun), green (physical strength), red (strength), blue (emotional healing)

GEMSTONES: agate, amazonite, bloodstone

METAL: gold

HERBS: agrimony, aloe vera, angelica, ash, basil, blackberry, centaury, chamomile, chilli, cinnamon, comfrey, dandelion, echinacea, eucalyptus, frankincense, garlic, ginseng, juniper, lemon balm, oats, olive, peony, pine, rose, rosemary, sage, sandalwood, willow, willowherb, yarrow

SYMBOLS: sun, ankh, caduceus, spiral, triskele

DEITIES: Apollo, Aesculapius, Sonzwaphi, Anahit, Aušrinė, Airmed, Atepomarus, Brigid, Dian Cecht, Sirona, Bao Sheng Da Di, Hua Tuo, Sekhmet, Isis, Cabuyaran, Akasi, Chiron, Aceso, Aegle, Panacea, Dhanvantari, Sukunahikona, Ninkarrak, Eir, Eshmun, Żywie

Abundance Spells

PLANET: Jupiter or sun

ELEMENT: earth

DAY: Thursday

MOON: waxing

COLOUR: green

GEMSTONES: aventurine (attracts wealth), emerald, topaz, diamond, jade

METALS: gold, silver

HERBS: apple, basil, clover, date, fig, goldenrod, maize, oats, sage, sunflower, wheat

SYMBOLS: fish, coins, green man, corn, seeds, eggs

DEITIES: Lakshmi, Kubera, Ganesha, Nang Kwak, Aje, Plutus, Veles, Juno Moneta, Abundantia, Odin, Ops, Sors, Fortuna, Horus, Renenutet, Tsai Shen, Toutatis, Caishen

Success Spells

PLANET: Jupiter

DAY: Thursday

MOON: waxing

COLOUR: orange

GEMSTONES: chrysoprase, topaz

METAL: tin

HERBS: date, fig, goldenrod, mandrake, nasturtium, orange

SYMBOLS: key, sun, arrow (direction/swiftness), crown

DEITIES: Jupiter, Zeus, Apollo, Helios, Mars, Ares, Hermes, Mercury, Ganesha, Lakshmi

Protection Spells

PLANET: sun

DAY: Sunday

MOON: full

COLOURS: blue, white, gold

GEMSTONES: amber (against the evil eye and enchantment), amethyst (against psychic attack), coral (against the evil eye), flint (against evil spirits and nightmares), haematite, jade, jasper (nightmares), jet

METAL: gold

HERBS: angelica, birch, black pepper, cedar, chamomile, chilli, cinnamon, clove, garlic, ginger, ginseng, gorse, hazel, heather, holly, houseleek, hyssop, ivy, lemon, mandrake, mistletoe, nasturtium, nettle, oak, olive, peony, rosemary, rowan, rue, sage, sandalwood, St. John's wort, thyme, turmeric, yarrow

SYMBOLS: arrowhead, eye, sword, mirror, witch ball, pentacle, valknut, hand of Fatima

DEITIES: Apollo, Kwan Yin, Athene, Freya, Bast, Brighid, Green Tara, Artemis, Diana, Empanda, Salus, Heimdall, the Dagda

Peace and Harmony Spells

PLANET: Venus

DAY: Friday

MOON: waxing, just full

COLOUR: white

GEMSTONES: amethyst (promotes harmony), beryl (harmony between couples), blue lace agate (inner peace), citrine (inner peace), sapphire (peace of mind)

METAL: copper

HERBS: basil, begonia, catnip, chamomile, coriander, date, dill, fenugreek, hazel, jasmine, lavender, lemon verbena, linden, olive, passionflower, rose, sandalwood

SYMBOLS: dove, dove feathers, olive branch, peace sign, yin/yang

DEITIES: Harmonia, Iris, Hestia, Vesta, Pax, Eirene

Good Luck Spells

PLANET: Jupiter

DAY: Thursday

MOON: waxing

COLOUR: blue

GEMSTONES: amethyst, Apache teardrop, aquamarine (for exams and interviews), carnelian, jade

METAL: tin

HERBS: basil, catnip, clove, clover, date, fig, fuchsia, goldenrod, gorse, hazel, heather, houseleek, jasmine, mandrake, oats, olive, orange, primrose, sunflower, turmeric

SYMBOLS: horseshoe, wishbone, four-leaf clover, fish, elephant

DEITIES: Fortuna, Lakshmi, Ganesha, Felicitas, Freya, Bes, Mercury

Communication Spells

PLANET: Mercury

DAY: Wednesday

MOON: waxing, full

COLOUR: yellow

GEMSTONES: topaz, jade, alexandrite, tourmaline, aquamarine

METAL: aluminium

HERBS: anise, benzoin, bergamot, caraway, clary sage, dill, eucalyptus, fennel, fenugreek, lavender, lemon verbena, lemongrass, marjoram, mint

SYMBOLS: feathers, envelopes, writing materials

DEITIES: Hermes, Mercury, Thoth, Ogma

Courage Spells

PLANET: Mars

DAY: Tuesday

MOON: waxing, just full

COLOUR: red/orange

GEMSTONES: carnelian, crazy lace agate, bloodstone, sapphire

METALS: iron, steel

HERBS: ash, basil, bay, cedar, centaury, cinnamon, clove, dragon's blood, fennel, frankincense holly, horseradish, madder, mustard, nasturtium, nettle, oak, orange, sunflower

SYMBOLS: teeth, claws, sword

DEITIES: Mars, Ares, Dagda, Herakles, Durga

Forgiveness Spells

PLANETS: Saturn, Neptune

DAY: Saturday

MOON: waning

COLOUR: violet

GEMSTONES: garnet, sodalite, Apache teardrop

METAL: platinum

HERBS: angelica, basil, centaury, chamomile, echinacea, elder, frankincense lavender, lemon balm, olive, rose

SYMBOLS: dove, scarab, frog, hummingbird, lizard, scissors (if the bonds are to be cut)

DEITIES: Kwan Yin, Concordia, Harmonia

Fertility Spells

PLANETS: moon, earth

DAY: Monday

MOON: waxing, full

COLOURS: white (moon), green (earth)

GEMSTONES: unakite, jade, carnelian, green aventurine

METAL: copper

HERBS: almond nut, apple, beechnuts, birch, catnip, cherry, date, grapevine, hazelnut, horse chestnut, linden, liquorice, maize, oak, oats, pinecone, pomegranate, sunflower seeds, turmeric, wheat grains, wild lettuce

SYMBOLS: frog, fish, goat, ram, bull, egg, seeds, seashell, thyrsus

DEITIES: Oshun, Hathor, Isis, Taweret, Coatlicue, Pachamama, Anahit, Parvati, Kichijōten, Brigid, Freya, Frey, Bona Dea, Juno, Venus, Aphrodite, Živa, Bes, Dis Pater, Min, Mylitta

Psychic Development Spells

PLANET: moon

DAY: Monday

MOON: full

COLOUR: white

GEMSTONES: moonstone, aquamarine (for clairvoyance and psychic dreams), beryl (stimulates visionary capacities), cairngorm (visions), carbuncle (peace of mind), sapphire (spiritual enlightenment)

METAL: silver

HERBS: acacia, bergamot. clary sage, cornflower, echinacea, lotus, mugwort, rue, vervain, yarrow

SYMBOLS: moon, bat, badger, bear, divination tools, crystal ball

DEITIES: Brighid, Hecate, Isis, Hermes, Thoth, Heka, Circe, Freya, Selene

Binding Spells

PLANET: Saturn

DAY: Saturday

MOON: waning

COLOUR: black

GEMSTONES: jet, slate

METAL: lead

HERBS: bindweed, cleavers, honeysuckle, willow

SYMBOLS: hourglass, knot, cord

DEITIES: Saturn, Cronos, Spider Woman, Athene, Minerva, Fates

Banishing Spells

PLANET: Saturn

DAY: Saturday

MOON: waning

COLOUR: black

GEMSTONES: black tourmaline, rutilated quartz, black obsidian, jet

METAL: lead

HERBS: asafoetida, avens, basil, beans, birch, garlic, hellebore, horseradish, juniper, marshmallow, rue, St. John's wort

SYMBOLS: bell, scythe, broom

DEITIES: Saturn, Cronos, Hecate, Ishtar, Kali, Shiva, Neith, Ptah

CHAPTER 18

· · · · · · · · · · · · · · ·

Talismans and Amulets

A talisman is a portable spell, designed to be worn or carried. It can take many forms, from an engraved metal disc to a painted piece of wood or bone, an inscribed piece of paper, a bracelet, a ring, or a scrip and so on. Talismans are often inscribed with the spell (or a symbol of it, such as a rune) they are designed to perform, and then charged and consecrated to possess specific energies, a function that the user knows so that, when it is in use, it evokes those powers. As it is named, it is given a symbolic birth by bringing it out of darkness into light.

$$\rightsquigarrow\!\!\!\!\!\!\!\!\!\!\!\!\ell\ell\ell\ell\ell\ell\ell\sim$$

Intent

Decide what the talisman is for. Why do you need it? What do you want it to do for you? Decide whether it is to be used for an active power like attracting good luck or is it to be a passive talisman for defending against bad luck, for example. In the first instance, you might choose a symbol of luck, such as a four-leaf clover, or in the latter, a shield. It is usual to give the talisman a name that reflects its purpose, such as defender, or joy bringer, and so on—the name should reflect its function. Naming the talisman emphasises it uniqueness, made for a specific person at a specific time and place for a specific purpose. The talisman has its own personality.

Preparation

If possible, the talisman should be made by hand. You might not be able to make silver jewellery, but you might be able to paint or burn a symbol into wood or write it onto paper. You should use materials that correspond to the purpose and desired outcome (see correspondences in the appendices). It should be made and consecrated at a suitable time. A talisman for growth might be made at the waxing moon, for example, while one for protection should be made at the full moon.

Visualisation

Now it is time to put the talisman together. As you make the talisman, it is important that you maintain concentration and visualise the desired outcome throughout the process. This focuses your intent into the object. When the talisman is finished, wrap it in a dark cloth or put it in a box so that it is enclosed in darkness.

Charging

You might charge the talisman at the same time you make it or wait and charge it when the next suitable time becomes available. Take the box you have put your talisman in, or the cloth you have wrapped it in, place it on your altar, and rotate it three times.

Unwrap the talisman to bring it out into the light in a symbolic act of birth. To reinforce this, you now give it a name. Sprinkle it with water and say,

> By *the power of water, I name you* [name].

Pass it over the candle flame (be careful if it is a flammable material) and say,

> By *the power of fire*, [name], *I give you life.*

Pass it over the incense and say,

> By *the power of air*, [name], *I give you your purpose* [speak the purpose].

Lay it on the dish of earth and say,

> By *the power of earth, you have been brought out of the darkness into light. I charge you, [name], to do my will. This rite is ended. Blessed be.*

Afterward

The talisman is now ready, fully empowered. When it is carried or worn, it reminds the user of its purpose and radiates the power of the ingredients and magic used to create it.

Amulets

An amulet—or good luck charm—is used to protect its owner. Unlike a talisman, it works via its inherent powers and is not consecrated. It is usually a natural object, such as a fossil or stone, feather, bone, or tooth that connect to animal powers, though an amulet can also be a small representation of an animal or god, even rosary beads or religious medals.

Herbal Amulets

Some plants have strong protective properties that can be used in personal warding magic.

ALDER: carry alder cones when you need strength

BEANS, DRIED: carry against witchcraft and the evil eye

BEECH: use beech bark in protective charms and amulets to place yourself under the shield of the goddess

CEDAR: carry a piece when you need protection

CLOVES: a necklace or pouch of cloves is protective

COMFREY: protection when travelling; put some in your shoe, place a piece in your suitcase, or hang some in your car

FLAXSEEDS: carry to ward off the evil eye and magical attack

HAZEL: carry hazelnuts for luck and protection

HEATHER: wear a sprig of heather when you need protection

ROSEMARY: carry a sprig or put some leaves into a small pouch and carry it for protection

SANDALWOOD: carry a piece of sandalwood for protection

Conclusion

If you have worked through this book from beginning to end, you will have gained greater insight into the path of the hearth witch and started to forge your own deep and fulfilling connections with the sacred.

True knowledge only comes from experience, and on our path, Mother Nature is the teacher. Witchcraft is watching the sunrise or sunset, the forest in the light of a glowing moon, or a meadow enchanted by the first light of day. It is the morning dew on the petals of a flower, the gentle caress of a warm summer breeze upon your skin, or the warmth of the summer sun on your face and feeling the underlying divine powers of the universe beneath all these things.

Witchcraft is experiential, personal, and unscripted. Its deepest secrets are printed nowhere; you must discover them for yourself. Everyone must learn their own magic, and only in this way shall you become wise, and truly call yourself a witch.

APPENDIX 1

. . . .

Elemental Correspondences

EARTH

The powers of earth are concerned with what is manifest, the material, the fixed, the solid, the practical, with what is rooted. Earth magic is concerned with manifestation, business, health, practicality, wealth, stability, grounding and centring, fertility and agriculture.

CARDINAL POINT: north

COLOUR: green

TOOL: pentacle

SYMBOLS: crystals, fur, coins, stone, bone, mirror, shield, tree

GEMS: green moss agate, emerald, green jasper, jet, malachite, olivine, peridot, green tourmaline, turquoise

METALS: lead, iron

HERBS: patchouli, vervain, honeysuckle, mugwort, fern, vetiver, primrose, hore-hound

AIR

The powers of air are concerned with the intellect, powers of the mind, knowledge (as opposed to wisdom), logic, inspiration, information, teaching, memory, thought, and communication. Inhaled air is the sustaining breath of life, while exhaled air carries the words, poetry, and song that communicate human ideas and knowledge. Air magic is usually concerned with the intellectual or the spiritual, the nontangible affecting the tangible, psychism, mental ability, protection, prophecy, and visualization.

CARDINAL POINT: east

COLOUR: yellow

TOOL: athame (or the wand, in some traditions)

SYMBOLS: eggs, feathers, sword

GEMS: topaz, aventurine, mica, fluorite, citrine

METAL: tin

HERBS: lavender, lemongrass, verbena, marjoram, mint, acacia, almond, benzoin, gum mastic

FIRE

Fire is the most mysterious of all the elements. It seems almost supernatural in comparison to earth, air, or water, which are states of matter, while fire is energy. Fire magic is concerned with creativity, life energy, and zeal. Fire gives us vitality, igniting action, animation, and movement. It sparks courage and acts of bravery. It heats passion and enthusiasm. Fire is the power of inner sight and creative vision, directing and controlling it to make it manifest in the world. It is concerned with the magic of active energy, illumination, wisdom, willpower, passion, and healing.

CARDINAL POINT: south

COLOUR: red

TOOL: wand (or the athame in some traditions)

SYMBOLS: candles, torches

METALS: brass, gold

GEMS: red agate, amber, bloodstone, carnelian, citrine, quartz, diamond, garnet, red jasper, lava, ruby, sard, sardonyx, sunstone, topaz, red tourmaline

HERBS: allspice, frankincense, ginger, juniper, marigold, orange, rosemary, dragon's blood, clove, bay, ash

WATER

Water is a liquid, like the blood that flows through our veins. It is associated with the emotions, feelings, and subconscious, and water magic is usually concerned with divination and scrying.

CARDINAL POINT: west

COLOUR: blue

TOOL: cup

SYMBOLS: cup, cauldron, pool, mirror, seashells

STONES: pearl, aquamarine, moonstone

METALS: quicksilver, silver

HERBS: aloe, apple, lemon balm, belladonna, birch, poplar, poppy, blackberry, burdock, camphor, chamomile, elder, ragwort, rose, coltsfoot, comfrey, daisy, daffodil, datura, sandalwood, yarrow, elm, eucalyptus, foxglove, hemlock, hemp, hibiscus, jasmine, yew, spearmint, thyme, kava kava, ladies slipper, lemon, myrrh, morning glory, passionflower

APPENDIX 2

Planetary Correspondences

SUN

DAY: Sunday

KEYWORDS: expansive, dynamic, male, abundance, health, illumination, creative, warmth, leadership, consciousness, vitality, stamina, healing, abundance, prosperity, protection

DEITIES: Apollo, Helios, Sol, Shamash, Ra, Amaterasu, Brigit

SYMBOLS: hexagon, sun, spiral, rayed shapes, fire in all its forms

COLOURS: gold, yellow

HERBS: herbs ruled by the sun turn toward the sun or have yellow flowers, like marigold, St. John's wort, and dandelion

METALS: gold, gold-coloured alloys

GEMSTONES: topaz, tiger's eye, citrine, yellow jasper, chrysoberyl

MAGIC: The sun's gift is warmth, light, and energy. It governs the pattern of life; its cycles divide the hours, days, months, and years, the round of sowing, growth, harvest, and decay. Sun magic is concerned with restoring vitality, health, and enthusiasm for life with abundance and creativity. Use it when you are feeling low and run-down to feel whole and fully alive and to restore energy and mood. On a higher level, the sun is enlightenment and spiritual understanding. It is the light in your soul that connects you to the soul light in all other beings. The energy of the sun is within your soul, ever present, waiting to shine.

MARS

DAY: Tuesday

KEYWORDS: dynamic energy, courage, strength, daring, aggression, sex, action, desire, competition, courage, passion

DEITIES: Mars, Ares, Durga, Tui

SYMBOLS: sword, shield, spear, pentagon

COLOURS: red, orange-red

HERBS: Mars plants symbolise a warlike spirit and generally have thorns or stings, like thistles and nettles, holly, ginger, mustard, cumin

METALS: iron, steel, nickel

GEMSTONES: red jasper, ruby, garnet, red agate, bloodstone, lodestone

MAGIC: Mars is the planet of assertive directed energy. You have the free will to follow the path and be happy, make a career off it and crash, or sit where you are and complain that life is passing you by. Use Mars energy when you need to take a good look at who you are, what you believe, and where you are going. Mars is the ultimate planet of action. Mars magic may be concerned with removing obstacles and building courage, strength, and passion, with motivation and willpower and achieving your goals.

SATURN

DAY: Saturday

KEYWORDS: constriction, limitation, aging, endings, death, crystallisation, structure, law, restriction, discipline, responsibility, obligation, ambition

DEITIES: Saturn, Chronos, Ea, Kali

SYMBOLS: scythe, keys, hourglass, triangle

COLOURS: black, grey

HERBS: Saturn plants are slow growing or long living and woody, thrive in the shade, have deep roots, or are poisonous, foul smelling, or considered evil, such as hemlock and henbane, yew, elm, cypress, pomegranate, violet, white lily, belladonna, mullein, opium poppy, myrrh, patchouli

METALS: lead, antimony

GEMSTONES: jet, black onyx, diamond, basalt, slate, obsidian

MAGIC: Saturn is the planet of endings, bindings, boundaries, and the crystallisation of efforts. The material world is transitory, and life is ephemeral, existing as it does in a time that passes. Time will destroy all, prince and pauper, priest and warrior, city and state. Saturn magic signals an end, an absolute transition from one state to another with no possibility of return. We experience many deaths in our lives as various stages and experiences end to make way for new phases and experiences, up until the ultimate transformation of physical death and rebirth. The old self dies so that a new self may be born. It can be very painful as the old self is stripped away and the birth pangs of the new self are felt. Saturn magic is concerned with building solid foundations through disciplined work, which some may view as restrictive, but which pays off in the long run, gaining profound wisdom and the skills of a master along the way. Saturn magic is also concerned with setting boundaries, with binding magic, with ending things you want to be rid of in a very definite way.

MERCURY

DAY: Wednesday

KEYWORDS: intellect, communication, travel, learning, analysis, mind, reason, language

DEITIES: Mercury, Hermes, Ogma, Thoth, Athena, Maat, Metis

SYMBOLS: caduceus, pen, octagon, feathers, books

COLOURS: orange, yellow

HERBS: Mercury is the planet of communication, so Mercury plants include fast-growing weeds, creepers and winding plants, or plants with hairy, fuzzy, or finely divided leaves; they may be aromatic

METALS: mercury, aluminium

GEMSTONES: carnelian, cairngorm, sard, banded agate

MAGIC: Mercury is the planet of thought and communication. It is named after Mercury/Hermes, the messenger of the Gods who crosses the boundaries between the worlds without hindrance, the patron of inventors, music, racing, and the alphabet, as well as numbers and weights and measures for merchants. Mercury energy combines thought and action and represents a burst of energy leading to lots of activity, travel, and getting things done. Mercury magic is performed when you want to open your mind to new ideas, when you want to study, and when you want to communicate and get your message or ideas out into the world. It is also the planet of travel, so Mercury magic can help in achieving your travelling goals.

VENUS

DAY: Friday

KEYWORDS: joy, benign, kind, concord, harmony, feminine, creative, harmonious and loving energy, attraction, love, relationships, art, beauty

DEITIES: Venus, Aphrodite, Ishtar, Freya, Bast, Hathor, Eos, Cupid

SYMBOLS: seashells, mirror, heptagon, sea salt

COLOURS: turquoise, green

HERBS: Venus is the planet of love and beauty, so Venus plants overwhelm the senses with sweet scents and lovely flowers, red fruits, or soft, furry leaves

METALS: copper, bronze

GEMSTONES: green jade, rose quartz, emerald, malachite, peridot, amazonite, coral, pearl, mother-of-pearl

MAGIC: Venus is the planet of love, and Venus magic is concerned with love in all its forms, from passion to friendship, connection with community, and compassion for your fellow beings. The power of love makes you feel more alive and that everything is more sharply in focus, every colour brighter and every sound more beautiful. The ancient Greeks thought that the very first divine being who emerged from primordial chaos—and the whole driving force behind creation—was love, which bound spirit and matter together, creating the world from opposites. Loving unconditionally reconciles your internal conflicts and creates the inner harmony that brings you closer to the oneness that is union with the divine. Venus magic includes magic of harmony and peace, pleasure, and artistic expression that comes from the heart.

MOON

DAY: Monday

KEYWORDS: the tides, subtle, feminine and inward-looking energy, changing, cold, intense, dreaming, unconsciousness, emotions, instincts, habits, moods

DEITIES: Diana, Artemis, Selene, Khonsu, Sin

SYMBOLS: bow, sickle, crystal ball, black mirror

COLOURS: silver, white, lilac

HERBS: The moon rules the instinct, emotions, and psychic abilities, and moon plants often grow near water or have a high water content or juicy leaves; they may have white flowers or moon-shaped leaves or seedpods

METALS: silver, platinum

GEMSTONES: moonstone, rock crystal, beryl, alabaster, alexandrite, fluorspar, selenite

MAGIC: The moon is the planet of the deepest feminine mysteries, imagination, visions, and dreams, which cannot be accessed by action or understood by logic. Spiritual insight springs from your subconscious, and its quiet voice speaks a different language, communicating in symbols and metaphors. This can only happen when the chatter of the thinking mind is stilled. While the rational, conscious mind is bright like the sun, the intuitive, unconscious mind is like the softer reflected light of the moon. The moon can give you many gifts, such as art, inspiration, spiritual insight, intuition, psychic skills, and visions. Use the magic of the moon when you need to turn away from outward concerns and look inward.

JUPITER

DAY: Thursday

KEYWORDS: benign, expansive, optimistic, benevolent, leadership, joy, abundance, luck, growth, expansion, optimism, abundance, understanding

DEITIES: Jupiter, Zeus, Thor, Odin

SYMBOLS: cornucopia, oak leaves, square

COLOURS: blue, lilac

HERBS: Jupiter is the bringer of abundance, so Jupiter plants are usually big and bold and often edible

METALS: tin, zinc, antimony

GEMSTONES: aquamarine, sapphire, lapis lazuli, amethyst, turquoise

MAGIC: Jupiter is the planet of abundance and expansion, so Jupiter magic is concerned with increasing your health, prosperity, and abundance. Use it for good things you want to grow, whether it be a business, more luck, more adventures, more life-affirming experiences, or even your understanding and personal philosophy. Always remember that you are asking for expansion of something that already has a beginning (however small), not for something to start from scratch, when using Jupiter magic.

URANUS

DAY: Tuesday

KEYWORDS: inspiration, invention, intuition, rebellion, liberation, sudden change, chaos, anarchy, freedom, awakening, revolution

DEITIES: Ouranos, Nuit, Urania

SYMBOLS: stormwater, the tower struck by lightning

COLOURS: violet, turquoise

HERBS: wild carrot, true unicorn root, spikenard, mugwort, skullcap, valerian

METAL: platinum

GEMSTONES: clear quartz, diamond

MAGIC: Uranus is a higher vibration of the planet Mercury. Mercury governs personal intellect, but Uranus expands to the collective consciousness. It takes the old, the structures and dogmas we have built, breaks them down, and makes them into something new. Uranus magic can be the lightning flash of truth that leaves your world in turmoil, but where you are forcibly reshaped. The process may be surprising, painful, and chaotic, but it gives rise to new insights and new directions. Uranus magic may involve embarking on dream quests, summoning visons, astral travel, and so on.

NEPTUNE

DAY: Thursday

KEYWORDS: passive, visionary, dreams, intuition, mysticism, imagination, delusions, dissolving, dissipation, glamour, illusions, disillusionment, transcendence, surrender.

DEITIES: Neptune, Poseidon, Amphitrite, Llyr

SYMBOLS: sand, sea salt

COLOURS: indigo, grey

HERBS: water lily, lotus, cucumber, melon, lilies, mugwort, silene capensis, ayahuasca, poppy, psilocybin, valerian

METALS: bronze, iron, pewter

GEMSTONES: clear quartz, smoky quartz, pearl, sapphire, amethyst, jade

MAGIC: Neptune is a higher vibration of the planet Venus. Rather than individual love, Neptune is the planet of universal love and compassion. Neptune is a planet of inspiration, dreams, psychic receptivity, spirituality, and illusions.

PLUTO

DAY: Tuesday

KEYWORDS: sex, transformation, power, death, rebirth, evolution, destruction, regeneration

DEITIES: Pluto, Hades, Yama, Persephone, Osiris, Dionysus, Kali

SYMBOLS: key, multiheaded animals, sceptre, pomegranate

COLOURS: dark red, metallic black

HERBS: the herbs of Pluto are moist and potent, either in their effect or scent

METALS: uranium, plutonium, platinum

GEMSTONES: snowflake obsidian, howlite, black tourmaline, smoky quartz, obsidian, topaz, ruby

MAGIC: Pluto is a planet of transformation, destruction and renewal, death and rebirth, the cycles of life that are forever creating, destroying, and creating again. Sometimes, we have to destroy parts of our lives, parts of ourselves, that no longer serve to be renewed, like a phoenix rising from the ashes. Pluto is a higher vibration of the planet Mars, but whereas Mars is concerned with physical strength and desire, Pluto is about the power of the soul. Its magic can be a powerful agent of fundamental endings and beginnings, shamanic dismemberment and reconstruction, spiritual insights, deeper truths, and connection with the higher soul after the death of the ego.

APPENDIX 3

. . . .

Metal Correspondences

COPPER

PLANET: Venus

QUALITIES: the power of connection

MAGICAL USES: love, sensuality, friendship, luck in love, beauty, art, balance, harmony, peace

GOLD

PLANET: sun

QUALITIES: riches, rulership, truth

MAGICAL USES: wisdom, longevity, moneys, depression, strengthening, wealth, protection, healing, authority, self-confidence, creativity, hope, power

IRON

PLANET: Mars

QUALITIES: iron and steel have been used for tools and weapons, working power and defence

MAGICAL USES: energy, strength, determination, willpower, aggression, speed, power, courage, assertiveness, protection, self-defence, wards

LEAD

PLANET: Saturn

QUALITIES: limitations

MAGICAL USES: cursing, time, the underworld, breaking bad habits and addictions

SILVER

PLANETARY RULER: moon

QUALITIES: rhythms, femininity, cycles, emotions

MAGICAL USES: moon goddesses, the female force, cycles, emotions, dreams, intuition, psychic work, fertility, protection, peace

TIN

PLANET: Jupiter

QUALITIES: abundance, growth, regeneration

MAGICAL USES: abundance, prosperity, energy, healing, regeneration, rejuvenation, wealth, wisdom

APPENDIX 4
. . . .
Colour Correspondences

BLACK: banishing, repelling, death, endings, destruction, winding down, the elderly, ancestor contact, the void or womb, receptivity, reincarnation, rejection of ego, possibilities waiting to be realised, Samhain, crone goddesses and death deities, the planets Saturn and earth, Scorpio and Capricorn, lead.

BLUE, LIGHT: physical health, loyalty, creative expression, tranquillity, peace, calm, harmony, protection, healing, spiritual development, teaching, luck, justice, autumn equinox, spiritual protection, throat charka, moon, water/air spirits, the planet Jupiter, the element of water, Virgo and Aquarius, tin.

BLUE, DARK: mental health, change, protection, spiritual protection.

BROWN: grounding, stability, earthiness, sexuality, practicality, environmental awareness, the planet earth, autumn equinox, Mother Earth and nature deities.

GOLD: stimulates awareness of spiritual connection, a melding of vital force and consciousness, happiness, rejuvenation, spiritual strength, spiritual zest, service to others, friendship, healing, energy, spiritual energy, strength, life force, solar plexus chakra, sun and corn deities, Midsummer, the sun, gold metal, faith and constancy, summer.

GREEN: regenerative, balancing, healing, equanimity, fertility, growth, prosperity, wealth, money, creativity, love, attraction, art, music, change and balance, Beltane, Yule, earth magic, compassion, heart chakra, Mother Earth, fairies, dryads, vegetation deities, the planet Venus, the element of earth, Venus, Cancer, Capricorn, Friday, spring, water, copper.

GREY: communication, study, teaching, divination, the planet Mercury.

INDIGO: perceptiveness, vision, intuition, insight, third eye chakra, Taurus.

MAGENTA: compassion, purifies and stimulates, aura enhancing, emotional equanimity, vision, creativity, insight, inspiration, creative vitality.

ORANGE: strengthens the will, aids the assimilation of new ideas, stimulates sexual energies, warmth, constructive vitality, optimism, success, courage, bravery, energy, ambition, luck, career, legal matters, self-esteem, spleen chakra, Samhain, Lughnasa, sun, Leo.

PINK: love, romance, friendship, happiness, harmony, peace, compassion, handfastings, beauty, heart charka, love goddesses, Libra.

PURPLE: strength, mastery, power, occult power, protection, Pisces, crone goddesses, Mercury, quicksilver, temperance, prudence, Sagittarius, winter, Wednesday.

RED: the gift of life, blood, vitality, warmth, stimulating energy and heat, willpower, courage, life, energy, libido, passion, lust, conflict, competition, strength, health, root chakra, Yule, Midsummer, fire spirits, mother goddesses, warrior Gods, the planet Mars, the element of fire, Aries, Cancer, iron.

SILVER: intuition, truth, enlightenment, agriculture, the home, medicine, psychic ability, removes negativity, communication, personal enlightenment, moon rituals, moon goddesses.

TURQUOISE: soothing, quieting, contemplation spaces, inventiveness, conception, philosophy, creativity, communication, throat chakra.

VIOLET: enhances highest spiritual aspirations, purity, high-frequency energy, transmutation, spiritual healing, mastery, ceremony, spirituality, self-respect, spiritual growth, spiritual fulfilment, self-esteem, third eye chakra, crown charka, Sagittarius.

WHITE: peace, cleansing, defensive magic, protection, purity, harmony, spirit, psychic development, the dispelling of negativity, purification, tranquillity, Imbolc, maiden goddesses, waxing moon, crown chakra, moon, silver, Monday, hope, innocence, Scorpio, Pisces.

YELLOW: joy, clarity, brightness, intellectual development, strength of mind, learning, study, eloquence, joy, air spirits, vision, solar plexus chakra, the planet Mercury, the element of air, Ostara, the planet Leo.

APPENDIX 5
· · · · · · · · · · · · · · ·
Gemstone Correspondences

ABUNDANCE

AMAZONITE: opening yourself to the flow of abundance

AVENTURINE: wealth, amplifies luck

BLOODSTONE: protection, resilience

CITRINE: welcomes abundance into your life, manifestation, prosperity

CLEAR QUARTZ: amplifies all

EMERALD: feeling abundance

GARNET: attracts good things

GREEN MOSS AGATE: wealth

JADE: attracting good things to flow toward you, prosperity and luck

LAPIS LAZULI: prosperity

MOONSTONE: new beginning

PERIDOT: moves things in the right direction

PYRITE: growth, good luck

ROSE QUARTZ: experiencing the flow of abundance

SAPPHIRE: prosperity

SELENITE: attracts positive energy

SODALITE: positive thinking

LOVE

AMETHYST: mending a broken heart

AVENTURINE: attracting new love, attracting romance, success

BLUE AGATE: harmony

BLUE CALCITE: attracting new love

CARNELIAN: passion

CHRYSOCOLLA: attracting new love, expressing love

GARNET: loyalty, passion

KUNZITE: loving and stable relationships

LAPIS LAZULI: loyalty

MALACHITE: attracting romance

MOONSTONE: loyalty, reuniting lovers

PINK TOURMALINE: attraction

PREHNITE: attracting new love

RED AGATE: passion

RED JASPER: passion

RUBY: sensuality, sexuality

Harmony and Peace

AMETHYST: peace and tranquillity, calming

BLACK OBSIDIAN: peace of mind

BLUE AGATE: harmony

CELESTITE: creating peace and happiness

CITRINE: grounds negative energy, soothes family problems, and promotes harmony

DESERT ROSE: improves love and harmony

HAEMATITE: clears away any negative feelings

HOWLITE: calms anger

JADE: joy and harmony

JASPER: alleviates stress, promotes tranquillity

ROSE QUARTZ: heals emotional wounds, cultivates love and harmony, encourages love and trust

TIGER'S EYE: creates understanding and calmness

TURQUOISE: soothes emotions

Compassion

APOPHYLLITE: clears the mind and body of negative debris

AQUAMARINE: calms the heart, tranquillity

MANGANO CALCITE: inner peace, pure love

OCEAN JASPER: expands the heart chakra, emotional stability

PINK OPAL: expands the heart chakra

RHODOCHROSITE: expands the heart chakra, healing emotional wounds

RHODONITE: stimulates the heart chakra

ROSE CALCITE: emotional healing, cleanses the heart chakra

ROSE QUARTZ: love for all, unconditional love, harmony, divine love, compassion

SMITHSONITE: calms emotions and connects to heart chakra

SUNSTONE: expands the heart chakra

CONFIDENCE AND COURAGE

AGATE: self-confidence

AMAZONITE: soothes the nervous system

AVENTURINE: helps with feelings of self-doubt and encourages optimism

BLOODSTONE: motivation and energy

CHRYSOCOLLA: courage in your own voice, especially for public speaking

CITRINE: optimism

DESERT ROSE: projects confidence

KYANITE: confidence in self-expression

MOONSTONE: inner strength and growth

PYRITE: confidence, manifesting your will

RED GARNET: courage

ROSE QUARTZ: raises self-confidence

RUBY: confidence

TIGER'S EYE: provides motivation and lessens fear, extra strength during difficult times

TOURMALINE: brings strength, diminishes fear

FORGIVENESS

AMETHYST: mending a broken heart

CHRYSOCOLLA: promotes calmness and a level head

MALACHITE: transformation and positive change

RAINBOW OBSIDIAN: brings hope and energy into blocked emotions

RHODONITE: forgiveness, moving forward, healing after trauma and grief

COMMUNICATION

APATITE: social ease and calm communication

AQUAMARINE: clear and calm communication

AZURITE: inner strength, clearing the throat chakra

CHRYSOCOLLA: stimulating the throat chakra to communicate effectively

LABRADORITE: communication

LAPIS LAZULI: communication, connects with the throat chakra

SODALITE: creativity, speaking your truth

TOPAZ: unblocking the throat chakra for clear communication

STUDY

PYRITE: activate intellect and memory

HAEMATITE: improves mental organisation

CLEAR QUARTZ: stimulates mental alertness

FLUORITE: clearing a confused mind

JOY

CALCITE: amplifies energy, positive thinking, motivation

CARNELIAN: success

CITRINE: warmth, joy, sparking enthusiasm, creativity

GARNET: warming the heart, recovering a sense of vitality

JADE: joy and harmony

PROTECTION

AGATE: protection while travelling

AMETHYST: blocks negative energies, protection from nightmares, protection against fear and anxiety

BLACK KYANITE: protects from energy vampires

BLACK OBSIDIAN: personal energy guardian, absorbs negativity and protects against it

BLACK TOURMALINE: blocks psychic attacks, clears negativity

CITRINE: wards off negative energy, grounds negative energy, emotional shield against spite and jealousy

CLEAR QUARTZ: clears away negative energy, deflecting negativity

EMERALD: protects the heart from hurt

HAEMATITE: shield from negative energy

JADE: protection against illness

MALACHITE: absorbs negative energies

OBSIDIAN: protective, absorbs negativity, shields against negativity, blocks psychic attacks

PYRITE: aura protection

SMOKY QUARTZ: blocks negative energies and earths them

TIGER'S EYE: wards off any malicious intentions

Home Purification

BLACK TOURMALINE: protection against negative energy and electromagnetic frequencies

CLEAR QUARTZ: clears away any negative energy, boosts immunity

PYRITE: detoxes energy from electrical devices

SELENITE: cleanses and purifies

SMOKY QUARTZ: grounding, protection from electromagnetic currents

Spiritual Work

AMETHYST: crown/third eye chakra, intuition, psychic ability, spiritual healing, meditation

ANGELITE: raising spirituality, soothing the soul

CARNELIAN: remove the fear of death

CELESTINE: dream recall, spiritual connection, connected to higher realms, meditation

CLEAR QUARTZ: open crown chakra, connection to higher self, clear mind, meditation

DESERT ROSE: enhances meditation, past-life work

FLUORITE: determining your life path, stimulating the third eye

IOLITE: third eye chakra, inner strength

KYANITE: shifts emotional blocks, dream recall

LABRADORITE: transformation, balancing the chakras, protecting the aura

LAPIS LAZULI: spiritual enlightenment, self-expression, truth

LEPIDOLITE: restore balance, awareness, clearing the chakras, balance

OBSIDIAN: stimulates growth, clarity, truth enhancing

OPAL: spiritual light to your aura, healing, raising cosmic consciousness

ROSE QUARTZ: healing emotional wounds, cultivating divine love, compassion

SELENITE: spirituality, healing, harmony, third eye, energetic master healer

SHUNGITE: quiet the mind and help with grounding

TITANIUM AURA QUARTZ: grounding and centring

HEALING

AMETHYST: healing and purifying

BLOODSTONE: improve circulation, blood-related issues

CARNELIAN: metabolism, menopause

CITRINE: health, removes toxic energy

CLEAR QUARTZ: master healer, supports the entire energetic system

JASPER: nurturing and supporting

OBSIDIAN: emotional healing

SELENITE: promotes harmony of hormone cycles, an energetic master healer

SUNSTONE: health and energy

TOURMALINE: good for digestive system, bones, and teeth

APPENDIX 6

Magical Herb Substitutions

LOVE

Apple
Basil
Broom
Calendula
Caraway
Cardamom
Carnation
Catmint
Cherry
Chickweed
Chilli
Cinnamon
Clove
Coltsfoot

Coriander
Cornflower
Cumin
Daisy
Damiana
Date
Dill
Dittany Of Crete
Fenugreek
Fig
Frankincense
Fuchsia
Geranium
Ginger

Ginseng
Goldenrod
Gorse
Hawthorn
Honeysuckle
Houseleek
Jasmine
Lavender
Lemon balm
Lemongrass
Lily
Linden
Liquorice
Lovage

Mallow
Mandrake
Meadowsweet
Mistletoe
Myrrh
Nettle
Orange

Oregano
Passionflower
Pomegranate
Poppy
Primrose
Rose
Rosemary

Saffron
Sweet cicely
Valerian
Violet
Wild lettuce
Yarrow

PASSION

Cardamom
Cinnamon
Coriander
Damiana
Date
Dittany of Crete
Fig
Frankincense

Garlic
Ginger
Ginseng
Houseleek
Iris
Jasmine
Mandrake
Myrrh

Pomegranate
Saffron
Sweet cicely
Thyme
Turmeric
Wild lettuce

HANDFASTING

Almond blossom
Anise
Apple
Broom
Cardamom
Cinnamon
Clove
Coriander
Cumin
Dill

Hawthorn flowers
Lavender
Mallow
Marjoram
Meadowsweet
Myrtle
Orange blossom
Oregano
Patchouli
Pomegranate

Poppy
Rose
Rosemary
Rue
Saffron
Skullcap
Sorrel
Strawberry
Turmeric
Violet

FRIENDSHIP

Begonia
Cardamom
Carnation

Catmint
Linden
Oregano

Passionflower

Compassion
Linden

Lotus

Healing

Agrimony

Aloe vera

Angelica

Apple

Ash

Basil

Bay

Blackberry

Centaury

Chamomile

Chilli

Cinnamon

Comfrey

Dandelion

Dock

Echinacea

Elder

Eucalyptus

Frankincense

Garlic

Ginseng

Hollyhock

Juniper

Lavender

Lemon balm

Oats

Olive

Peony

Pine

Rose

Rosemary

Sage

Sandalwood

Sassafras

Willow

Willowherb

Yarrow

Abundance

Apple

Basil

Bergamot

Clover

Cloves

Date

Fenugreek

Fig

Goldenrod

Maize

Mandrake

Oak

Oats

Orange

Pomegranate

Rose geranium

Sage

Sunflower

Turmeric

Wheat

Money Drawing

Basil

Bergamot

Cloves

Date

Fenugreek

Goldenrod

Maize

Mandrake

Oak

Oats

Orange

Pomegranate

Turmeric

SUCCESS

Date
Fig

Goldenrod
Mandrake

Nasturtium
Orange

LUCK

Basil
Catnip
Clove
Clover
Date
Fig
Fuchsia

Goldenrod
Gorse
Hazel
Heather (white)
Houseleek
Jasmine
Mandrake

Oats
Olive
Orange
Primrose
Sunflower
Turmeric

FERTILITY

Almond nut
Apple
Beechnuts
Birch
Catnip
Cherry
Date

Grapevine
Hazelnut
Horse chestnut
Linden
Liquorice
Maize
Oak

Oats
Pinecone
Pomegranate
Sunflower seeds
Turmeric
Wheat grains
Wild lettuce

PEACE

Basil
Begonia
Catnip
Chamomile
Cloves
Coltsfoot
Coriander
Date

Dill
Fenugreek
Hazel
Jasmine
Lavender
Lemon verbena
Linden
Maize

Mistletoe
Oat
Olive
Passionflower
Rose
Sandalwood
Valerian

VISIONS

Clary sage
Coltsfoot
Damiana

Lemon balm
Lotus
Mugwort

Mullein
Poppy
Rue

Vervain

Wild lettuce

Willow

Yarrow

CLAIRVOYANCE

Acacia

Bergamot

Clary sage

Cornflower

Echinacea

Lotus

Rue

Vervain

Yarrow

Bay

Belladonna

Bistort

Calendula

Camphor

Chicory

Cinnamon

Clary sage

Cleavers

Damiana

Dandelion

Fern

Flax

Hazel

Hemp

Honeysuckle

Lemongrass

Linden

Mace

Mugwort

Mullein

Nettle

Nutmeg

Oats

Orange

Poppy

Rowan

Saffron

Sandalwood

Vervain

Wild lettuce

Wormwood

Yarrow

DIVINATION

Alder

Almond

Aloe

Anise

Apple

Ash

PSYCHIC AWARENESS

Aloe

Angelica

Anise

Bay

Bearberry

Benzoin

Borage

Dandelion

Eyebright

Henbane

Myrrh

Smallage

MEDITATION AND RELAXATION

Acacia

Benzoin

Bergamot

Chamomile

Feverfew

Frankincense

Hollyhock

Horse chestnut

Lavender

Lemon balm

Patchouli

Rose

Sandalwood

Skullcap

Renewal

Alder	Heather	Violet
Almond	Ivy	Willow
Chamomile	Lilac	Willowherb
Cinnamon	Parsley	
Cleavers	Rose	

Protection

Acacia	Daisy	Hyssop
Agrimony	Dill	Iris
Alder	Dittany of Crete	Ivy
Aloe vera	Echinacea	Lemon
Anemone	Elder	Lemongrass
Angelica	Elm	Lily
Basil	Eucalyptus	Linden
Beech	Fennel	Liquorice
Birch	Fenugreek	Lovage
Black pepper	Feverfew	Mallow
Bluebell	Fig	Mandrake
Broom	Flax	Mint
Calendula	Foxglove	Mistletoe
Caraway	Garlic	Mugwort
Carnation	Geranium	Mullein
Cedar	Ginger	Nasturtium
Centaury	Ginseng	Nettle
Chamomile	Gorse	Oak
Chickweed	Hawthorn	Olive
Chilli	Hazel	Peony
Cinnamon	Heather	Pomegranate
Clove	Holly	Primrose
Cohosh	Honeysuckle	Rosemary
Comfrey	Horehound	Rowan
Coriander	Horsetail	Rue
Cornflower	Houseleek	Sage

Sandalwood

St. John's wort

Thyme

Turmeric

Valerian

Willow

Yarrow

Apotropaic

Acacia

Anemone

Ash

Basil

Bean

Birch

Broom

Cedar

Centaury

Chamomile

Eucalyptus

Fenugreek

Feverfew

Fig

Frankincense

Garlic

Hazel

Heather

Hyssop

Juniper

Lavender

Lemon

Lilac

Mugwort

Pomegranate

St. John's wort

Thyme

Valerian

Yarrow

Exorcism

Asafoetida

Avens

Basil

Beans

Birch

Garlic

Hellebore

Horseradish

Juniper

Marshmallow

Rue

St. John's wort

Counter Magic

Chilli

Date

Dill

Honeysuckle

Horehound

Nettle

Peony

St. John's wort

Binding

Bindweed

Cleavers

Honeysuckle

Willow

Cleansing and Purification

Agrimony

Angelica

Avens

Basil

Bay

Bean

Beech

Benzoin

Birch

Broom
Burdock
Camphor
Caraway
Cinquefoil
Clove
Comfrey
Dill
Dragon's blood
Eucalyptus
Fennel

Frankincense
Gorse
Garlic
Horehound (white)
Hyssop
Juniper
Lavender
Lemon balm
Lovage
Nettle
Oak

Pine
Primrose
Rosemary
Rue
Sage
Soapwort
St. John's wort
Tansy
Thyme
Vervain

Aura Cleansing

Agrimony
Angelica
Bean
Betony

Cinquefoil
Fumitory
Horehound
Jasmine

Rosemary
Sage

Consecration

Bay
Bayberry
Belladonna
Bindweed
Borage
Calendula
Caraway

Chicory
Clover
Dragon's blood
Frankincense
Fumitory
Hemlock
Horehound

Hyssop
Mint
Nettle
Olive
Rue
Sunflower

New Moon

Aloe
Birch
Blackberry
Camphor
Clover

Daisy
Gorse
Ground ivy
Jasmine
Lily

Mulberry
Ox-eye daisy
White rose
Wormwood

WAXING MOON

Aloe

Camphor

Cinquefoil

Lily

Mugwort

Ox-eye daisy

Poppy

Rose (white)

FULL MOON

Alecost

Avens

Bindweed

Birch

Blackberry

Chervil

Cinquefoil

Clover (white)

Cornflower

Dandelion

Fir

Frankincense

Hawthorn

Jasmine

Lady's mantle

Marshmallow

Mugwort

Periwinkle

Poppy

Rose (red)

Strawberry

Sweet cicely

Vine

Woodruff

WANING MOON

Aspen

Blackberry

Clover

Cohosh (black)

Elder

Garlic

Henbane

Myrrh

Parsley

Willow

DARK MOON

Anemone

Bean

Bindweed

Blackthorn

Cypress

Elder

Elm

Foxglove

Garlic

Grape

Heather (white)

Juniper

Lilac

Lily

Mint

Myrrh

Parsley

Pomegranate

Poplar

Violet

Willow

Yew

APPENDIX 7
· · · · · · · · · · · · ·
Magical Ingredients for Food

APPLE: love, fertility, abundance

APRICOT: love

BANANA: fertility

BASIL: blessing, peace, harmony, abundance

BLACK PEPPER: protection, courage

CABBAGE: peace

CARDAMON: lust, love, harmony, attractiveness

CARRAWAY: fidelity, retention

CHERRY: love, lust, fertility

CHILLI: love, aphrodisiac

CHOCOLATE: love

CLOVES: protection, love, prosperity

CORIANDER: love, passion

CUMIN: love, faithfulness, fidelity

DATE: aphrodisiac, potency, virility, love, fertility

DILL: love, peace, harmony

FENNEL: fertility, courage, joy

FIG: Prosperity, fertility, lust

GARLIC: strength, courage, aphrodisiac

GOOSEBERRY: fertility

GRAINS: abundance

GRAPE: fertility, prosperity

HAZELNUT: wisdom

HONEY: healing, love, fellowship

LEMON: love, happiness

LEMON BALM: joy

LENTIL: peace, tranquillity

LETTUCE: peace, tranquillity

LIQUORICE: love, fidelity

MARJORAM: peace, harmony, love, tranquillity

MULBERRY: fertility

NUTS: fertility, love, prosperity

OLIVE: wisdom, fertility, power

ONION: protection, cleansing, healing

ORANGE: fertility, love, luck, happiness, prosperity

OREGANO: joy, love, happiness

PAPAYA: love

PARSLEY: rebirth, renewal

PASSIONFRUIT: peace, harmony, love

PEACH: love, fertility

PEAR: abundance, prosperity

PEAS: abundance

PLUM: love

POMEGRANATE: fertility, passionate love

QUINCE: love

RADISH: lust

RAISIN: fertility

RASPBERRY: love

RHUBARB: love

ROSEMARY: marriage, remembrance, healing, love

SAFFRON: aphrodisiac, marriage, love

SAGE: wisdom

SALT: protection, wealth

SESAME: fertility, prosperity

STRAWBERRY: love

THYME: courage, aphrodisiac

VANILLA: lust, love

APPENDIX 8

· · · · · · · · · · · · ·

Herbs for Home Warding

ACORNS: hung in windows, acorns protect the house from lightning.

AGRIMONY: wards off negative energies or spirits, blocks curses and magical attacks, returning them to their sender. Employ as incense/ritual fumigation, hang some in the home, or add to herbal amulets.

ALOE VERA: hang a leaf of aloe vera above your front door for protection and keep a plant in your kitchen.

ANEMONE: hang a bunch of anemones on outbuildings and stables to protect them and the animals within.

ANGELICA: used to seal doors and windows against negative influences.

BASIL: deflects negative energy; wards off harmful spiritual energies, evil spirits, black magic, and psychic attacks.

BIRCHWOOD: used to make protective wards.

BLUEBELL: flowers in the bedroom will keep away nightmares.

BROOM: repels negativity.

CALENDULA: use in protection oils and powders or grow in pots around the home.

CARNATION: use in protection incense, scrips, and talismans.

CARRAWAY: seal doors and windows with caraway oil.

CEDAR: burn cedar incense or essential oil in the bedroom to prevent nightmares (extinguish it before you go to sleep). Hang some above the door and windows of your house to repel negativity.

CENTAURY: use in incenses and charms to repel evil.

CHAMOMILE: chamomile oil smeared around doors and windows prevents negativity entering. Plant in the garden as a guardian herb.

CHILLI: hang a string of dried chillies in your kitchen as a protective charm or put a wreath of chillies on your front door.

CINNAMON: use in incenses, potions, scrips, rituals, and spells for protection.

COHOSH, BLACK: powdered root can be sprinkled around a room or across the threshold for protection and to dispel negative influences.

DAISY: Use in herbal talismans of protection. Place a daisy chain in a child's bedroom for protection.

DILL: used to counter magical attack and negative energy; dill oil can be used to seal protective talismans, doorways, and so on, or simply hang the seed heads in the home.

DITTANY OF CRETE: use in incenses, spells, herbal talismans, and so on for protection.

ECHINACEA: adds strength to scrips, incenses, and spells of protection.

ELDER: carry the wood and twigs for protection or hang some in the home.

FENNEL: use fennel oil to magically seal doorways and windows to prevent evil from entering.

FEVERFEW: use a macerated oil smeared around your doors and windows to keep out negativity.

FLAX: seeds may be scattered on the threshold of your house for protection or scattered around your bed if you are suffering from nightmares sent against you.

FOXGLOVE: growing foxglove will protect the home and garden. Grow one near the door to repel evil influences. Use the leaves in protective talismans and wards hung around the house.

GARLIC: hang up in the home to ward off negativity and the evil eye. Cloves of garlic may be placed in protective charms and wards.

GERANIUM, SCENTED: use for protection in oils and charms.

GINGER: use ginger oil/infusion to seal talismans of protection and the root in protection incense.

HAWTHORN: warding magic, protection amulets, and protection oils and incense.

HEATHER: heather twigs are used to make brooms and besoms with magical powers of protection.

HOLLY: protection against lightning, bewitchment, and evil spirits. Plant a holly tree near the front door, place holly branches and leaves in the windows, or use a holly wand to banish. A sprig in the bedroom protects against nightmares.

HONEYSUCKLE: grow honeysuckle around your door or use in incense, protection oils, or talismans.

HOREHOUND, WHITE: hang a sprig in the house; use in protection oils and herbal amulets.

HORSETAIL: can be employed in spells, incense, amulets, and pouches for strength and protection.

HOUSELEEK: will give good protection to those in its sphere of influence. Grow it on the roof of the house, shed, or garage, in cracks in pavements, rock gardens, or pots and baskets by the front door.

HYSSOP: hung in small bunches above windows and doorways will protect the property and prevent any negative energy from entering.

IRIS: root and leaves can be hung about the home and added to the bathwater for personal protection.

IVY, ENGLISH: grow up your garden walls or on the house to safeguard your property. Place sheafs of ivy near your front door or hang an ivy wreath on it.

LEMON: repels the evil eye by sympathetic magic. Lemons can be hung in the home or outside the front door. Add dried peels to protective scrips and charms.

LINDEN: hang linden branches over doorways; plant a linden tree in the garden; add the dried flowers to incenses, herbal amulets, and wards.

LIQUORICE: offers protection from negative energy. For this, it may be powdered and sprinkled about the house in doorways and windows.

LOVAGE: hang above your doors and windows to keep negative energies out or plant in the garden to protect it.

MINT: hung in the home or used in scrips and protection amulets.

MISTLETOE: used as a protection against lightning, disease, fires, and misfortunes.

MULLEIN: protection from negative influences and evil spirits. Hang it in your house or place it beneath your pillow to prevent nightmares. Use a mullein oil to magically seal your doors, windows, and property to prevent negative energy entering.

NASTURTIUM: plant a red nasturtium by your front door to deter unwanted visitors and keep negative influences from your home.

NETTLE: ward off negative entities and protect the home from the effects of storms.

ORRIS: the root powder may be sprinkled about the home.

PEONY: petals may be scattered around thresholds and the dried petals and powdered root used in protective incenses. Grow peony in your garden, put the dried petals in potpourri or scrips, or carry on the person in herbal talismans. Place a peony scrip under the pillow to prevent nightmares.

POMEGRANATE: drives out negative energies and wards off evil spirits. Place pomegranates in vulnerable areas.

PRIMROSE: use an infused primrose oil for sealing doors and windows against negative influences.

ROSEMARY: hang a wreath of rosemary on the front door and some sprigs over the windows. If you suffer from nightmares, place a sprig beneath your pillow.

ROWAN: berries or wood can be used in an incense to banish undesirable entities. Plant a protective rowan near your house.

ST. JOHN'S WORT: protective and countering magic. Hang small bunches under the eaves or in the windows of the home to keep away evil spirits and render spells sent against you useless.

THYME: may be hung around the house and placed in scrips. Wear thyme to ward off negativity and evil.

VALERIAN: protection against evil. Grow some in the garden or hang the root in the home to protect it from negativity and evil influences.

YARROW: add to incenses, scrips, and spells.

APPENDIX 9

· · · · · · · · · · · · ·

Fumigation Herbs

ACACIA RESIN: repels negativity and evil

ANGELICA: purifies a person or space

BENZOIN RESIN: cleanses and purifies

BIRCH: cleanses and purifies

CEDAR: purifies the working area and magical tools

DILL: cleanses an angry atmosphere

EUCALYPTUS: purification of a home, sacred space, or aura

FRANKINCENSE: cleanses, purifies, consecrates, drives away negativity

GINGER: cleansing tools and magical spaces

HEATHER: clears negativity

JUNIPER: purifies, banishes negative spirits

LAVENDER: purifies and cleanses

MUGWORT: cleanses negativity

ROSEMARY: protects and cleanses

SAGE: cleanses negativity

SAGE, GARDEN: purifies spaces; cleanses the aura, the working area, and magical tools

VERVAIN: cleanses the aura

BANISHING/EXORCISM FUMIGATION HERBS

AGRIMONY: wards off evil spirits

CENTAURY: dispels negativity, repels evil, exorcism

CHILLI: repels evil spirits

GARLIC: exorcism

HAWTHORN: exorcism, protection

HOREHOUND: sacred space and aura cleansing, exorcism

PEONY: exorcism

ROWANBERRIES OR WOOD: banishes undesirable entities

RUE: banishes negative energies, exorcism, purification

ST. JOHN'S WORT: repels negativity, purifications, exorcism

Bibliography

Anderson, Miranda. *The Book of the Mirror: An Interdisciplinary Collection Exploring the Cultural Story of the Mirror*. Cambridge Scholars Publishing, 2007.

Arnold, James. *Country Crafts*. John Baker, 1968.

Baker, Margaret. *Folklore and Customs of Rural England*. David and Charles, 1974.

Blackburn, Bonnie, and Leofranc Holford-Strevens. *Oxford Companion to the Year*. Oxford University Press, 1999.

Blagrave, Joseph. *Astrological Practice of Physick*. N.p., 1671.

Cambell, Joseph. *The Masks of God*. Penguin, 1976.

Colquhoun, Ithell. *The Living Stones: Cornwall*. Peter Owen, 1957.

Culpeper's Complete Herbal. W. Foulsham and Co., n.d.

Davies, Owen. *Popular Magic: Cunning-Folk in English History*. Continuum, 2007.

De Cleene, Marcel, and Marie Claire Lejeune. *Compendium of Symbolic and Ritual Plants in Europe*. Man and Culture Publishers, 2003.

De Menezes, Patricia. *Crafts from the Countryside*. Hamlyn, 1981.

Evans, Alex. *The Myth Gap*. Penguin, 2017.

Farrar, Janet, and Stewart Farrar. *Spells and How They Work*. Robert Hale, 1990.

Fortune, Dion. *Applied Magic*. The Aquarian Press, 1981.

Glanvill, Joseph. *Saducismus Triumphatus, or Evidence Concerning Witches and Apparitions*. N.p., 1681.

Gordon, Lesley. *A Country Herbal*. Peerage Books, 1980.

Hjalmar Öhrvall. *About Knots*. Albert Bonnier, 1916.

Hoggard, Brian. *Magical House Protection: The Archaeology of Counter-Witchcraft*. Berghahn Books, 2019.

Hole, Christina. *Witchcraft in Britain*. Paladin, 1977.

Howard, Michael. *Scottish Witches and Warlocks*. Three Hands Press, 2013.

Howard, Michael. *Welsh Witches and Wizards*. Three Hands Press, 2006.

Lewis, John. *Early Greek Lawgivers*. Bristol Classical Press, 2007.

Logan, Jo. *The Prediction Book of Amulets and Talismans*. Javelin, 1986.

Mabey, Richard. *Plants with a Purpose*. Fontana, 1979.

Michell, John. *At the Centre of the World*. Thames and Hudson, 1994.

Newdick, Jane. *Sloe Gin and Beeswax*. Charles Letts and Co., 1993.

Peck, Harry Thurston. *Harpers Dictionary of Classical Antiquities*. Harper and Brothers, 1898.

Pennick, Nigel. *Secret Signs and Sigils*. Capall Bann, 1996.

Pennick, Nigel. *The Ancestral Power of Amulets, Talismans and Mascots, Folk Magic and Religion*. Destiny Books, 2021.

Ryall, Rhiannon. *West Country Wicca*. Capall Bann, 1998.

Sebastiani, Alrgaea. *By Rust of Nail and Prick of Thorn*. Amazon, 2017.

Seymour, John, and Sally Seymour. *Self Sufficiency*. Faber and Faber, 1973.

Sibley, Sian. *Unveiling the Green*. Black Lodge Publishing, 2022.

Soraya. *The Witch's Companion*. Waverley Books, 2011.

Stapley, Christina. *Herbcraft Naturally*. Heartsease Books, 1994.

Trumbull, H. Clay. *The Threshold Covenant*. Charles Scribner's Sons, 1896.

Uyldert, Mellie. *Metal Magic: The Esoteric Properties and Uses of Metals*. Turnstone Press, 1980.

Vickery, Roy. *Oxford Dictionary of Plant Lore*. Oxford University Press, 1995.

Walsh, Penny. *Spinning, Dyeing and Weaving*. New Holland Publishers, 2009.

Watts, D. C. *Elsevier's Dictionary of Plant Lore*. Elsevier, 2007.

Williams, David Lewis, and David Pearce. *The Neolithic Mind*. Thames and Hudson, 2005.

Notes

Notes

Notes

Notes

Notes

Notes

To Write to the Author

If you wish to contact the author or would like more information about this book, please write to the author in care of Llewellyn Worldwide Ltd. and we will forward your request. Both the author and the publisher appreciate hearing from you and learning of your enjoyment of this book and how it has helped you. Llewellyn Worldwide Ltd. cannot guarantee that every letter written to the author can be answered, but all will be forwarded. Please write to:

Anna Franklin
℅ Llewellyn Worldwide
2143 Wooddale Drive
Woodbury, MN 55125-2989
Please enclose a self-addressed stamped envelope for reply,
or $1.00 to cover costs. If outside the U.S.A., enclose
an international postal reply coupon.

Many of Llewellyn's authors have websites with additional information and resources. For more information, please visit our website at http://www.llewellyn.com.